Ju-Jitsu

JU-JITSU

Martin Dixon
seventh dan

The Crowood Press

First published in 2002 by
The Crowood Press Ltd
Ramsbury, Marlborough
Wiltshire SN8 2HR

www.crowood.com

British Library Cataloguing-in-Publication Data
A catalogue record for this book is available from the British Library.

ISBN 1 86126 455 0

Dedication
I dedicate this book to my wife Sheila and all my family.

Acknowledgements
Special thanks to my wife Sheila, my family and my students who
continue to support my work and put up with the occasional limits on
out time together. There would be no book without the dedicated,
wonderful team of Ju-jitsu teachers who work behind the scenes to
ensure that every single member is looked after. It would have been
wonderful to have every member of that team take a part in this book,
but physically that was impossible. Spiritually, however, they were all
there with me.

I would like to thank some of my students who were able to
participate in the photographs and gave up their valuable time. They are
Stuart Fletcher, Heath Blackledge, Tina Clarkson, Dean Angotti, Mark
Bridge, Lauren Bridge, Christopher Bridge, Anthony Smith, Sheila
Dixon, Janice Angotti, William Rogers and Derek Shaw.

Photography by the Garth Dawson Studio

Disclaimer
The author and publisher cannot accept responsibility for injuries or
damage arising from the application of techniques described in this
book. It is recommended that you consult a doctor before undertaking
any physical activity.

Throughout this book 'he', 'him' are used as neutral pronouns and as
such refer to both males and females.

Typeset by Naomi Lunn

Printed and bound in Great Britain by J W Arrowsmith, Bristol

Contents

Introduction

This book aims to explain the basic techniques of Ju-jitsu, in a manner that is easy to understand, along with an introduction to the philosophies and traditions that surround them. Its purpose is not to turn you into a fighting machine, but to inspire you to become a historian, an educator, a philosopher and a disciple of the code of Bushido.

All students of Ju-jitsu should ask themselves why they want to learn the art, and whether they are willing to be transformed and to live by Ju-jitsu's code of ethics. The journey towards an understanding of the art is a never-ending one, but, whatever the true meaning of its teachings, they come from the past to influence the future.

1 A Brief History of the Art

Origins

The term 'Ju-jitsu' is a generic one and is almost indefinable. It can be taken to be all-encompassing, as the roots of the art have developed from the use of weapons to weaponless systems of fighting, from defending against weapons to defending against unarmed and multiple attacks.

How old is the art of Ju-jitsu? Where did it begin? There are no clear answers to these questions, although there are many excellent reference books on the subject. It is generally believed, however, that many martial arts schools (ryu) were formed during the Edo period (1601–1867). During this period, commerce and industry developed rapidly. Merchants began to have more power than the Samurai. The schools tended to specialize in the use of only one weapon, and this became an acceptable practice. Most systems at the time depended upon the use of weapons and unarmed combat was only introduced much later. It was necessary at the time for a warrior to have about his person or in his possession an array of weapons, but the one weapon always associated with the Samurai is, of course, the sword, or katana (see pages 99–109, on weapons).

The wearing of armour and its design was changing rapidly in Japan, as in many other countries. The first designs for the mounted Samurai were heavy and very ornate. The common foot soldier, on the other hand, wore a very simple affair constructed out of small metal plates bound together with leather and wrapped around his body.

The use of the horse in battle declined as the Samurai's role changed and he was increasingly involved in defending encampments, and so on. The Samurai saw that the lighter version of the armour worn by the foot soldier would suit him much better for situations of field combat. This led to further improvements in the design of armour, until eventually the hotoke-do came to be the most popular. The surface of this armour was very smooth and the joints between the plates of metal were concealed. Obviously, trying to attack someone in full armour using kicking or punching methods was useless, as the armour was able to withstand heavy blows from sharp weapons. This, and the potential scenario of both combatants becoming disarmed, led to the development of grappling-type systems of fighting. These developing methods were most effective against an opponent in full armour. Systems began to be formulated and documented, and many clans, styles and unarmed combat systems began to emerge. This was surely the birth of many of the systems of Ju-jitsu that are still in use today.

Most martial arts can trace their ancestry back to a warrior monk called Daruma, who is believed to have travelled to Tibet and China studying the various methods of grappling. The first mention of Ju-jitsu was a reference from the history of the Edo period that dated from 1196 AD:

On this day the birthday of our Lord Kamakura, two Ken [Senior Samurai] demonstrated an advancement in unarmed grappling/combat. They call this method Ju-Jutsu. As the demonstration progressed it was evident that the Lord of Kamakura was most impressed at the new innovation. For, while we have seen traditional methods of Hakuda [grappling], this new form did consist of many strange movements of twisting and turning and locking of joints, as well as many strikes with open hands and the feet, and many grips with the fingers, which caused obvious pain. At the end of the demonstration my Lord Kamukara called the Samurai and engaged them to teach his house. Their names were Chojun Yoshensei from Kyoto and Genji Suzuki from Nagasaki.

These grappling systems emerged and flourished during the domestic peace of the Tokugawa Period. During the early 1800s, a number of groups in Japan favoured the deposition of the Tokugawa Shogunate and the ascension of an Emperor to the throne. Clans were the political parties of the time. The leader of the Aizu clan, Katamori Matsudaira, had served the Shogunate for many years and the loyalty of the Aizu clan therefore lay with the Shogun. The Aizu fought many battles in an attempt to keep the Emperor and his forces from the throne, and played a pivotal role in the Bakumatsu wars. The Choshu and Satsuma clans supported the Emperor and threatened the political lifestyle of the Aizu.

Saigo Tanomo and Takeda Sokaku

With their opposing ideologies, the Aizu Samurai, under the leadership of Saigo Tanomo (1830–1905), clashed against the forces of Choshu and Satsuma at Shirakawaguchi. Saigo Tanomo was an Aikijujutsu and Kenjutsu student under Takeda Soemon (1758–1853), had studied for years with the Takeda schools, and was a famous warrior. However, he suffered defeat at the hands of the Choshu and Satsuma clans. Following the defeat, twenty-one members of his family committed suicide, in the belief that Tanomo had been killed.

In fact, Saigo Tanomo had survived the battle of Shirakawaguchi. He returned to Aizu and became a teacher of Mizoguchi Ha Itto-Ryu and Koshu-Ryu Gungaku Kenjutsu. In 1876, he received a new student, Takeda Sokaku (1860–1943), into his tradition. Sokaku, grandson of Takeda Soemon, was born in Aizu and had studied Aikijujutsu with his grandfather and other arts with his father. By the time he was sixteen he had studied Jikishinkage-Ryu Kenjutsu from Sakakibara Kenkichi and received his Menkyo Kaiden in Ono Ha Itto-Ryu from Toma Shibuya of Tokyo. Saigo Tanomo remembered Sokaku's grandfather well, as he had also been taught by him. For three years Sokaku studied Daito-Ryu with Tanomo and mastered many arts, such as Aikijujutsu, Battojutsu, Yarijutsu and Kenjutsu. Finally, in 1880, at the Nikko Toshogu Shrine, Tanomo passed on all his knowledge, including the secret teachings, to Sokaku.

From that day forward, Takeda Sokaku would be headmaster of Daito-Ryu. For almost twenty years, he wandered from dojo to dojo, challenging every known martial arts master, and was never defeated. He took time in his travels to instruct others, often staying with the student for a period of time before moving on. He concentrated on government officials and military leaders as well as local police departments for his student body. In this manner his reputation spread quickly.

Kano Jigoro

In 1882 things began to change. In that year, Kano Jigoro founded a new type of Jujutsu that he called Judo. Kano was a Jujutsu master who had studied under Senseis Teinosuke Yagi and Hachinosuke Fukada of the Tenshin Shin'Yo-Ryu. Later he also studied under the tutelage of Tsunetoshi Iikubu of the Kito-Ryu, and for a while with the Sekiguchi-Ryu.

Kano was born in a small costal town outside of Kobe, Japan, in 1860. His main martial theories were developed by his study of the 'secret' books Hontai and Seiko, which discuss the fundamentals of nage (throwing) through the principle of ki-to (to raise up, to strike down). He combined his study of this with his grappling knowledge from the Tenshin Shin'Yo-Ryu, and retired to the solitude of the Eishoji Temple to develop his Judo. Kano's Jujutsu was distinguished by his approach to training. Because he sought to preserve the Jujutsu techniques, but realized that Jujutsu had a bad reputation, he changed the entire philosophy surrounding his art. Kano emphasized the physical fitness aspects of the art and altered the techniques, in order to make them appealing to the general public.

The sporting aspect of the art was also considered. Kano arranged Kata (prearranged forms) for the self-defence techniques in order to ensure safety and enjoyment in learning, but also retained shiai (contest) to test timing and technique in a semi-combat situation. Kano also invented the ranking system that consisted of kyu ranks (trainees) and dan ranks (graded). Before Kano, the ranking system had not existed. Kano also targeted government and military officials as his primary student population, and his Judo soon became widely popular.

Saigo Shiro

Kano's Judo achieved its fame because of Aikijujutsu. Kano was an excellent Jujutsuka himself, but felt that in order to prove that his new form was 'undefeatable' he would need to employ an 'undefeatable' representative. This man was Saigo Shida (1867–1922), who later changed his name to Saigo Shiro.

Shiro was the adopted son of Aikijujutsu master Saigo Tanomo, a master of Daito-Ryu at a young age and trained for the headmastership of the Takeda tradition. He was recruited by Kano to be his 'showman' for the Kodokan system and this is why Takeda Sokaku became Daito-Ryu's headmaster (see below). Shiro was known for his great ability and strength at a young age – he was a Godan (5th degree) by the age of 21. In the contests set up between the Kodokan and the area Jujutsu schools, Saigo easily defeated all opponents, mostly with his favourite technique Yama Arashi. Kodokan was 'proving' its worth by using Aikijujutsu, although most of the techniques Shiro used were never taught by Kano. Whereas Aikijujutsu had a thousand or more techniques, the Kodokan system boasted about 150.

After many years Saigo Shiro left the Kodokan and became a reporter and master of Kyudo (archery). Subsequently, the style moves into the realm of martial sport. Saigo Shiro, perhaps one of the world's greatest Jujutsuka, died on 23 December 1922 at the age of 57.

Developments Worldwide

By the turn of the 20th century, many of the koryu or 'ancient schools' were gone, or disappearing. It was the perfect time for Judo to come on strong. Kano made his Judo the standard physical education for the Japanese

Police Force and Army, and the sport was also popularized in the United States. In 1889 Kano had sent Yamashita Yoshiaki to the USA to live and to instruct Judo at Harvard University and at the Annapolis Academy. This had greatly enhanced the popularity of Judo with the new US audience. Even though Kano had, in fact, used Aikijujutsu to make his art famous, he did do Jujutsu a great service. Without the renewed interest in the grappling arts inspired by Judo there is a distinct possibility that Jujutsu would have never survived as a martial art. After an illustrious career, Kano died while travelling at sea in 1938. Today, Judo is practised all over the world and is an Olympic sport.

After the dissolution of the Samurai in the late 1800s, the Japanese began to have more frequent contact with the Americans. Not only was this America's first contact with Japanese culture, but one single event sparked interest in the minds of Americans about Japan's martial arts. In 1904 American teacher Charles Parry and Takeda Sokaku met on a train in Japan. There was an argument between them about their seats in the first-class section of the train, and Sokaku found it necessary to restrain the American, although Parry was much taller and bigger than he was. Amazed at how helpless he was against a man of less than five feet in height, Parry reported to his superiors in the USA on the great power of Aikijujutsu. President Roosevelt sent for an Aikijujutsu instructor to come to the USA and put on a formal demonstration of the art. Takeda sent Police Officer Shinzo Harade between 1904 and 1910, and the sport immediately gained great renown, and many students, including Charles Parry himself.

Takeda Sokaku died on 25 April 1943 at Amori Station in Honshu, leaving behind his great tradition to his son Takeda Tokimune and his senior students Hisa Takuma, Sagawa Yukiyoshi, Yamada Taisaburo, Matsuda Toyosaku, Yamamoto Kakuyoshi and Ueshiba Morihei. Takeda Tokimune currently teaches in Abaragi prefecture, Hokkaido, Japan.

At the end of the 1800s the Samurai were politically disbanded and many Jujutsu/Kenjutsu schools died out. The few Jujutsu schools that survived came in from the countryside to the city, and began to be exposed to other ryu. There were many contests between Jujutsu schools at the time, each trying to prove that it was the best. Many styles were defeated and discredited (some unjustly), and the schools were forced out of existence, as practitioners joined other ryu. Many of the younger students used their skills to bully unsuspecting city folk, starting bar brawls in order to show off their techniques. Jujutsu fell into ill repute, with many of its practitioners being seen as troublemakers, and the practice of Jujutsu was restricted to a very few traditional schools.

Daito-Ryu to Aikido

Ueshiba Morihei is widely known as the founder of Aikido. Born on 14 December 1883 to a farming family in an area of the Wakayama prefecture, now known as Tanabe, he was an only son with five sisters. As a young man he moved to Tokyo to study Kito-Ryu Jujutsu and Shinkage-Ryu Kenjutsu. Around 1903 he joined the military and served in the Russo-Japanese war.

Ueshiba was one of the senior students of Takeda Sokaku, grandmaster of Daito-Ryu Aiki Jutsu. He recognized that he was no match for his teacher, and threw himself into his training. Later, Ueshiba went to Shirataki to build a dojo and Sokaku came to live there at Ueshiba's invitation.

Takeda Sokaku was born the second son of Takeda Sokichi on 10 October 1859, in the Takeda mansion in Oike, Aizu. As a boy, he learned Kenjutsu, Bo Jutsu, Sumo and Daito-Ryu from his father, and studied Ono-Ha Itto-Ryu at the Yokikan dojo under Shibuya Toba. The Daito-Ryu scrolls were handed down to Sokaku and included a lineage tracing the art back to the Emperor Seiwa. (According to legend, the Emperor won his throne because his Sumo champion defeated the champion of his brother.)

The history of Daito-Ryu indicates that it was developed as a means of self-defence, specifically used inside the palace by warriors. The term oshikiiuchi, which appears in documents of the day, came to be loosely translated as 'honourable ceremony inside'. It became equated with the term gotenjutsu, or 'self-defence techniques for use within the palace'. Perhaps this is evidence of the defining links between the founding systems of Ju-jitsu and other arts.

Developments in Europe

Ju-jitsu came to the UK in the early 1900s when World Champion Sada Kazu Uyenishi first visited. He was a small man, with gold-rimmed spectacles, and many people found it hard to believe that he was capable of taking on and overcoming the many opponents who were put against him. Uyenishi had been encouraged to take up the art of Ken Jutsu, in which he later on became an expert, and then had gone on to study Ju-Jutsu in Osaka. He was not the most famous Ju-jitsu exponent of his time, but he soon became well known around the Aldershot area, training with the gymnastic staff at Shorecliffe Army camp. Many of the tech-niques taught by Sada Kazu Uyenishi in the UK were for a long time considered to be of a secret nature, with the various locks and throws generally being shown only to a select few.

By this time, Ju-jitsu was becoming an accepted method of combat or defence, which anyone could learn and in which anyone could become an 'expert'. A wealth of knowledge was coming into the West from men who had been serving overseas and had taken up these so-called 'forbidden arts' – certainly, Ju-jitsu was frowned upon after the war, when there was a preference for activities such as Judo, which were seen to be more sporting.

The general perception of the time was that anyone involved in combat arts, for example, wrestling, had to be big and strong. People were beginning to understand that this was not a requirement of Ju-jitsu. Time after time, challenge after challenge, European wrestlers were being beaten by much smaller and lighter opponents. Sada took on allcomers. Many famous fighters of the time, including Peter Gotz, Lauritz Nielsen, Charles Laurie, Bartoletti, Charles Wilson, Sergeant Judge and Sheki, one of his own countrymen, all failed to defeat him.

Sada's father, Kichibe Uyenishi, was a big, strong man – weighing 14 stone and standing six feet tall – in direct contrast to his son. He is known to have used his swimming skills one day in Belfast, when a man fell out of a boat. Uyenishi dived in and brought the unconscious man to shore. He then performed Japanese artificial respiration (raku) on the man and saved his life.

2   Ethics and Codes of Conduct

A Philosophical Perspective

Serious study of any martial art should include the development of a philosophical background. As a student develops his aptitude in Ju-jitsu, the interrelationship between the physical and mental aspects of the art should also be developed and strengthened. The result can be a philosophy that can have a profound influence on the daily life of the practitioner, with Ju-jitsu training at its base.

The deeper the knowledge and understanding of the art, the stronger the philosophy that goes with it. A number of factors need to be taken into consideration during the development of a philosophy:

- The dynamic, powerful and destructive potential of Ju-jitsu techniques from a purely physical viewpoint;
- The skilled control of the attacker's ki, the inner spirit, driving force or centre of energy. When a person commits to a course of action, he is using and committing his ki; in other words, all his energies are directed towards a particular end;
- Students need to develop a knowledge of the location and use of nerves and pressure points;
- Students need to develop the skill and knowledge to create and control pain, without doing any real harm to the attacker;
- These skills, combined with the ability to create real pain, which would disable most attackers, lead to a realization of the poten-

tial damage a Ju-jitsu exponent can inflict on an attacker;
- This destructive potential, inherent in all martial arts, emphasizes the concept of non-violence;
- Physical confrontation should be avoided whenever possible;
- As the Ju-jitsu student becomes more confident in his new-found skills he has an increased chance of being able to defend himself in a confrontational situation, but he should never need to prove this point;
- If a physical confrontation does occur, it could be said that all attempts at reasoning have been exhausted.

Everyone has the right to defend himself, but the Ju-jitsu practitioner must be guided by ethical motives, with the intention to defend himself without hurting others. He must respect the natural integrity of the opponent's anatomy. With practice, effective self-defence becomes possible without the necessity of inflicting serious injury upon an aggressor. True victory is only achieved if no one loses. The Ju-jitsu practitioner must be responsible for his own safety and the safety of those he is protecting, and for not inflicting unnecessary damage upon the aggressor.

There are basically four levels of ethical behaviour in combat, with associated ethical considerations:

1. An unprovoked attack with initiative, and without provocation, resulting in the injury or death of another person. This is

Ethics and Ju-Jitsu

(Reproduced by kind permission of the Ju-jitsu International Federation.)

According to an old saying pertaining to martial arts, 'One must first learn civility before he learns the art, and one must first know his ethics before he knows his skills.'

'Civility' in this context refers to good manners, courtesy, respect and consideration for others. The term 'ethics' refers to a fundamental set of acceptable behaviours, which codifies the spirit of martial arts. Martial artists can rely on this set of behaviours to cultivate their body and mind, and to guide their everyday actions and judgement. Ethics is an integral part of the study of martial arts, setting the moral guidelines for martial artists. The principles of ethics represent the traditional, cultural and social standards by which practitioners are trained in martial arts. Central to these principles are the concepts of non-violence, respect for self and others, loyalty to family and country, and the following of the natural way.

According to ethical principles, every individual has a moral obligation to society and his fellow human beings, as well as towards nature, which surrounds him. The concept also relates to the attitudes, lifestyle, and the social and moral behaviour of the martial arts practitioner, governing his behaviours, in both word and deed. A practitioner of martial arts should be a superior athlete, well versed in combat, but also an upstanding citizen with good moral and social virtues. The fulfilment of the ethical principles is the true spirit and ultimate goal of the way of martial arts, inspiring all less than perfect beings to strive continually for perfection within.

Today's personal and social challenges – in a climate of increasing violence and deteriorating ethical values – demand additional education and training beyond that of the academics. Individuals need to be taught the skills to resolve conflict peacefully and to build character. The martial arts offer much potential for this teaching. The art of Ju-jitsu can be an intelligent and effective way to prepare people to cope with today's challenges.

Aims of Training and Practice

Despite some false perceptions, Ju-jitsu is not a violent, military discipline. Instead, it is a means through which practitioners can come to understand and deal creatively with conflict. Traditionally, the study of Ju-jitsu involves both the practice of skills and an adherence to ethics. The skills learned from Ju-jitsu practice hone the physical body, sharpen the reflexes and strengthen the resolve, but these skills should always be counterbalanced by good conduct. The primary goal of the practitioner is to become a better, more understanding person, living with a greater expectation of a sincere life. With a vital role in the non-violent resolution of conflict, Ju-jitsu clearly has the potential to become a significant educational model for use in raising young people.

The philosophy behind Ju-jitsu involves the achievement of a life lived in peace, wisdom, morals, love and self-discipline through intellectual means. Ju-jitsu teaches certain virtues – humility, courage and integrity – which help to build a strong and honourable character, and contribute to a more peaceful and gentle world. The original martial arts of peace, which became over time the arts of war, have the potential to be peaceful and healing again, but only with the right vision and the means to carry out this vision.

Mental Attitude

A good quality of life requires health, both mental and physical. The art of Ju-jitsu cannot exist without the mental aspect, which is the foundation upon which physical improvements are built. Ju-jitsu is much more than just a workout. It is an alteration, both physically and mentally, of lifestyle, which will last a lifetime. Actions are brought together with thoughts; fighting is integrated with philosophy.

Worthwhile accomplishment in Ju-jitsu training is only achieved through dedication, effort and discipline. Every aspect of Ju-jitsu requires the harmonization of the mind and body. This harmonization is achieved through mental focus and concentration, combined with proper respiration and accurate physical techniques. The aim of Ju-jitsu training is the welfare of the practitioner. Self-defence skills are attained, but the focus should be on the individual's character development. The ability to practise self-defence greatly improves self-confidence. Self-confidence, combined with better judgement, integrity and overall improvement in lifestyle, brings a positive attitude. With physical skills as a base, the Ju-jitsu practitioner develops the confidence to use psychological and sociological self-defence skills, which enable him to deal with the fears and challenges of everyday life. A well-rounded personality can be realized only if the spirit is right.

Self-Restraint and Self-Control
Ju-jitsu practice is not a vehicle for the venting of anger, frustration or emotional problems. Serious Ju-jitsu practitioners must accept the philosophy of non-violence, and a physical confrontation should be avoided whenever possible. The use of force is condoned only in self-defence or in the defence of those who are defenceless. Meaningless rivalry, foolish stunts, the intimidation of others, violent behaviour, criminal activities, self-preening vanity, and any vices or addictions are not condoned. The Ju-jitsu practitioner displays courage in the use of his skills to satisfy the demands of ethics, and in defence of his country or fellow human being against unjust violence, to the point of supreme self-sacrifice, if necessary. The Ju-jitsu practitioner should use his knowledge only to protect himself and others from harm, and then only to the extent of protecting and removing himself from the situation.

If it is necessary to use Ju-jitsu against an adversary, the practitioner should use self-restraint and good judgement. A properly trained Ju-jitsu practitioner will do everything possible to avoid a physical confrontation, not only because he knows that such confrontation is unnecessary, but also because he knows that he has a better than average chance of successfully defending himself. A physical confrontation is philosophically degrading, as it indicates that all other means of avoidance have failed.

The Ju-jitsu practitioner should also adopt an attitude of self-control – he must 'bend like the willow'.

Self-restraint and self-control will help the Ju-jitsu practitioner to become a better person and, at the same time, to avoid unnecessary confrontations. This will be made possible because of the inner peace and confidence that the practitioner develops. Patience is the key.

Discipline is the exercising of self-control. In Ju-jitsu, it encompasses the emotions, actions and mental activities of the practitioner, and is one of the cornerstones from which mastery is attained.

Goals and Codes of Ethics
The stated goals of the popularization of Ju-jitsu and its ethics principles are as follows:

1. To promote and perpetuate the art of Ju-jitsu and to foster respect for its founders and their history, philosophy and principles.
2. To disseminate information to the martial arts community and the public about the art and science based upon practitioners' style of life and behaviour, their written notes and records, and through formal and informal meetings on these topics.
3. To serve as a living repository of all of the various aspects of Ju-jitsu, including physical–technical training, historical foundation, scientific basis and philosophical–mental spiritual learning.
4. To maintain high standards of presentation when addressing subjects related to Ju-jitsu, never falling into unnecessary arguments and comparisons, but always making reference to the moral values.
5. To give recognition to legitimate coaches and practitioners of Ju-jitsu.
6. To establish a Code of Ethics calling for mutual respect between members and for coaches and practitioners of other martial arts disciplines.

In order to achieve these goals, Ju-jitsu schools and clubs need highly trained coaches, with the necessary skills and resources to prepare their athletes to cope with the various challenges. If the art is to evolve from self-defence and competitive sport to a peaceful and spiritual discipline, with the wider mission of addressing the social and individual ills of humankind, training programmes and innovative curricula will need to be developed.

Coaches can have significant influence on developing athletes who rely on them for the instruction and guidance necessary to reach the top levels. Their power must not be abused, and they must follow a code of ethics and conduct, for the mutual benefit of all concerned. The criteria involved in the evalution of new teaching and training methodologies should be established according to the best interests of the athlete. Coaches must establish their end goals, the relationship of those goals to Ju-jitsu's code of ethics, and the means by which they are to be achieved.

Ju-jitsu coaches must be competent, always recognizing the limitations of their expertise. They must seek to promote integrity in their practice, and must be honest, fair and respectful of others. They should uphold professional standards of conduct, and accept personal and professional responsibility.

Personal Interpretations

Everyone has his own interpretation of the various terms used in Ju-jitsu practice, and they may differ to the point that converging efforts towards virtues and ethical principles may be jeopardized. In order to establish some common ground, some basic interpretations are given here. The aim is to pave the road for a smooth start, without limiting the freedom of the route to be pursued.

- Benevolence: 'I will look for the good in all people and make them feel worthwhile. I will show compassion to all living things and nature.'
- Character: 'I will reflect honour and respect on the martial arts and our forms of association by leading a clean and upstanding lifestyle. It is not through words, but my actions, that I will set a good example for others to follow.'
- Courage: 'I will develop courage by opposing influences that can cause failure and defeat mentally, physically and spiritually. I will stand up for the truth and justice. I will not display petty bravery by engaging in meaningless rivalry, foolish stunts or the intimidation of others.'
- Courtesy: 'I will extend proper manners and etiquette to those I meet.'
- Encouragement: 'I will be as enthusiastic about the success of others as I am about my own accomplishments.'
- Endurance: 'I will persevere through all obstacles and challenges in life. I will not lose faith in myself or those I love through physical, mental and emotional hardship.'
- Family dedication: 'I will continually work at developing love, happiness and loyalty in my family and acknowledge that no other success can compensate for failure in the home.'
- Forgiveness: 'I will forget the mistakes of the past and press on to greater achievements in the future.'
- Health: 'I will protect my skills by avoiding harmful health practices such as smoking, drugs and excessive use of alcohol. I will preserve and defend the ethics of Ju-jitsu and will never enhance my mental and physical performance unnaturally (nor treat ailments or injury when it is medically unjustified) for the sole purpose of taking part in a competition by using prohibited substances prior to or during a competition or a training.'
- Honesty: 'My personal, business, academic and family life will be conducted honestly, and will not accommodate lying, cheating or stealing.'

the lowest level and is ethically inexcusable and reprehensible;

2. The provocation of an attack by insult or a contemptuous attitude, then the injuring of the other person when he retaliates. The instigator is responsible for inciting the attack, and there is little ethical difference between this and the lowest level;

3. Defence against an unprovoked attack in which the attacker is injured or killed. Because the defender is not responsible for the attack, this is more defensible ethically than the lower levels; however, the result is the same – injury to or death of the other person;

4. Controlled defending against an unpro-

voked attack, in which neither attacker nor defender is injured. This is the ultimate ethical level of self-defence. It requires not only great skill, but also ethical motives and a sincere desire to defend oneself without hurting others. This is the goal of all true self-defence arts and must become the goal of all Ju-jitsu practitioners if they are to rise above their performance of physical techniques.

Years of continuous training and development of mental and physical skills result in the widening of the student's knowledge base. With repetition and self-testing in intricate forms, and with higher-graded Jujitsu exponents, he gradually becomes one with the art.

The ability to understand and control both one's own ki (or energy) and an attacker's ki is a third element affecting growth. Learned techniques should flow spontaneously from the centre of the body. The student can sense and use his attacker's ki only if he (the student) is relaxed. If the student can control his own ki it is possible for him to remain calm and in control of himself in stressful situations.

The environmental training of a student is a significant determining factor upon his perception of Ju-jitsu. Most people take up the art for self-defence, while others turn to it as a purely physical activity for fitness. Some are more interested in the esoteric side, which deals with relaxation and meditation. The most fulfilling approach is to become totally involved in all aspects. As the study progresses, the student begins to understand the relationship of techniques, why they are performed in certain ways, and how they relate to other aspects of everyday life.

In Ju-jitsu, all things must be in harmony. Even that which might be considered as random and chaotic in nature is revealed eventually as the highest form of organization. For every action there is a reaction. Pressure is not pressure unless it meets with resistance. Resistance is not resistance unless it has pressure placed upon it. The art of Jujitsu is not a study that takes many years but a continuous learning and experiencing curve. There is no 'journey's end', only the journey and its signposts along the way.

An awareness of the traditions and history of Ju-jitsu and martial arts in general is also important. As Ralph Waldo Emerson wrote, 'The years teach much which the days never know.' Many people who come to Ju-jitsu classes today have no concept of the traditions and philosophies that form the basis of the art. Teachers must be well versed in the history and pass it down to students, as they would have done in the past.

The training and traditions related to the ancient weapons of Ju-jitsu have associations that are more than relevant today: honour, respect, discipline, humility, gratitude and happiness. Surely these virtues are the bedrock for any decent society? Training in Ju-jitsu takes place within the context of teachings that have these philosophies at their core. Ju-jitsu teaches students much about social history, and not just the history of Japan, bringing to life traditions and principles in a form of self-defence.

A Transformational Process

On the surface, Ju-jitsu is just 'self-defence', but the practitioner must look deeper. Remember: the fish are not on the surface but in the water itself. Every practitioner should be willing to be transformed, to be altered for the better, not only physically, but also mentally, morally and spiritually.

In most societies, ethics and morality are not inborn due to local social conditions. A Ju-jitsu coach has the responsibility to include the teaching of such subjects in martial arts training, in order to produce Jitsuka to be proud of.

The martial arts are both philosophical and spiritual; it may sound contradictory to describe a method of fighting as such. In fact, Ju-jitsu is one of the most profoundly philosophical and spiritual disciplines, with the road to spiritual richness usually beginning with the reality of the body. It may be difficult to separate the philosophical from the spiritual practice, but the key to the philosophical practice of Ju-jitsu lies in the seeking or expression of higher wisdom and knowledge – in dealing with something beyond the purely physical, in order to attain higher awareness and broader consciousness.

The martial art of Ju-jitsu incorporates ideas such as the two universal realms (philosophical and spiritual) and the dual forces of life (called the yin and the yang by the Chinese). The art is used as a way to investigate such ideas, as an enquiry into life, bringing life to Ju-jitsu. For example, when you discover in your practice that being calm and centred helps the effectiveness of your martial techniques, you will want to explore the way in which this inner calm and outer action relate, and, further, how this relationship works in life in general outside the martial arts.

The martial arts can also be used to express ideas that the practitioner finds valuable, relating perhaps to beauty, harmony, control, assurance, and maybe even morality. In expressing such things, the practitioner might also be able to lift himself to a higher level of these qualities in his life.

In order to approach the spiritual aspect of the martial arts, it is necessary first to take the physical steps, as it is via the physical that it is possible to experience the spiritual. The martial arts practitioner must learn to become aware and intimate with the space around his body. Total body awareness allows you to move in a graceful, whole and integrated way, and to perform techniques with clarity and strength. This stage leads not only to effectiveness in the martial sense, but also to a perspective that allows a greater appreciation of some of the more eternal and universal qualities of life – efficiency, integration, creativity, patience, spiritedness and naturalness. These qualities come from the personal and spiritual side, yet also belong to the more universal domain. They are found at all times and in all places. They allow contact with a side of life that transcends the corporeal, the mundane, and the purely personal.

Harmony of mind, body and spirit starts here. The spiritual aspect deepens with practice and perseverance. Jitsuka should take time to savour and work on such spiritual qualities, without trying to 'force it' or seek to find them too soon.

Long-term involvement with Ju-jitsu teaches practitioners that the philosophical and spiritual aspects of the martial arts are the most important. Fighting is not as rewarding as peace, confrontation is not as satisfying as harmony, and separateness is not as meaningful as unity. Learning how to injure another human being leads to an awareness of the fragility of the human being – of the human condition – and to a sense of caring for that fragile life. In the light of the tender and sensitive balance of life, its preciousness becomes only too evident. Defeating another is not as important as compassion; overcoming another person is not as valuable as respect, and subduing someone else is not as important as helping.

Ju-jitsu teaches its practitioners that strength of body must be tempered with intelligence. The mind must be elevated and controlled with spirit, and the spirit is thereby strengthened with mind and body. Forcefulness is not as important as guidance.

The constant struggle for proper technique will show you how divided and unwhole the mind and body can be, and the importance of the integration and balance of mind, body and spirit. Integration leads to a smoothness and clear awareness; where there is no integration, awareness is dulled, and, when awareness is dulled, the capacity for enjoying life is diminished.

Through the application of energy in Ju-jitsu movements the individual further learns that appropriateness should take precedence over indiscriminate action. In order to become a good Ju-jitsu martial artist, it is necessary to endure difficulties, control temper, and be humble. Tolerance must also be developed, for in the martial arts there is much to test an individual's capacity for generosity and acceptance. Endurance, control, humility and tolerance are all sound spiritual qualities.

Dealing with movement and efficiency with such great subtlety gives an appreciation of naturalness, which should be highly prized and respected, and be a guiding principle.

Ju-jitsu students must also learn the meaning of etiquette (forms) and be aware of its origins. When acting with awareness with a mind of the real, it is clear that genuine and felt actions are the essential and true heart of an individual's motivations. Etiquette and ritual are symbolic expressions of real and authentic actions. In Ju-jitsu, students should learn the difference between empty ritual and sincere actions. This discovery of the true meaning behind ritual leads to genuine etiquette, which is etiquette with conviction. When this happens, the individual is beginning to delve deeply into the spiritual roots of Ju-jitsu, taking advantage of Ju-jitsu as a method of self-exploration and self-development.

Long-term commitment to Ju-jitsu can lead you to see the reality of the philosophical and spiritual in the martial way. These are not merely empty words, but real and tangible qualities, which can be approached with assurance. In addition, it is important to understand that the philosophical and the spiritual should be balanced and harmonized with other concerns such as health, self-defence and society. When the student has engaged with Ju-jitsu in these ways, is persevering, and has sincerity, he can be said to be an authentic Ju-jitsu practitioner.

Jitsuka must agree to live by the art's code of ethics. Any Ju-jitsu practitioner, school or club must serve as an example of this code in its daily life. The study of martial arts is an endless journey and an important element of life. Many benefits are derived from martial arts. Each practitioner's goal is to continue to improve the quality of his own life. The goal of each school and club is to improve the quality of life of its members and to share the benefits of the martial arts equally throughout society.

The point at which you decide to join this journey is up to you. If you choose the wrong teacher or club, you may also decide at some time on your journey that you want to get off. There are many closely guarded secrets within the martial arts and Ju-jitsu is no exception. They should not be revealed too soon in a student's development nor to someone who cannot be trusted.

Beginners should remember the saying, 'If you don't know, ask. You will be a fool for the moment, but a wise man for the rest of your life' (Seneca). Teachers should abide by the Chinese proverb, 'A thorn defends the Rose, Harming only those that would steal the blossom.'

Coming to a recognition that you can improve your own potential in Ju-jitsu is a transformational process. Surely one of the main objectives in life is to live to your full potential. Along this journey you should be developing your own human spirit and qualities such as humility, understanding, kindness, honesty, compassion, courage and dependability. The journey to develop these qualities is endless.

The key to success and happiness, whether it is training in Ju-jitsu or any other martial art, is the conscious control of thought and a continuous radiation of constructive thinking and acting.

3 Philosophy

Before joining a Ju-jitsu club you need to ask yourself certain questions. There are many reasons for taking up a martial art, from a need for self-defence to a simple desire for fitness, but the learning of Ju-jitsu requires a serious commitment. Remember, there is no beginning and no end on this continuous journey.

It is important to have some information about getting started in physical training, but it is also vital to understand what you may become. You need to accept that you can transform yourself if you want to. Every individual has his own interpretation of the philosophy of Ju-jitsu (see Chapter 1), but the most important thing is to recognize its significance. A student who builds on the philosophical foundations will go on to become a true martial artist.

Ju-jitsu and Personal Development

Ju-jitsu has the potential to enhance a Jitsuka's personal development. It is easy to become caught up in the complexity and confusion of modern society, and many people become influenced by material achievement and neglect personal growth. Such characteristics as greed, jealousy and a sedentary lifestyle are destructive and contradictory to the development of the martial artist's internal well-being. Ju-jitsu gives the student the focus and discipline actively to pursue the positive qualities needed for greater personal satisfaction. In a wider sense, it can give the practitioner the strength to improve this constantly changing world.

The true value of life will be recognized and enhanced only by a person who strives to improve himself from within. Education allows the individual to use his inner potential to become a professionally trained person. The Ju-jitsu practitioner should strive to improve himself and his abilities in the martial arts in order to serve others. Flowing out towards others will allow him to know himself and to grow, and, ultimately, to improve the quality of Ju-jitsu. Students and coaches should share pride in the development of the martial arts and open their mind to new ideas for improving and serving humanity. Jitsuka should be faithful to the ideals of Ju-jitsu and attempt to spread and develop these beliefs within the younger generations so that they too will be morally and physically fit. However, Ju-jitsu training should not be self-serving. Teaching only, without working out, feeds the ego.

An attitude of perseverance and patience is essential. Developing the younger generation into morally, physically and spiritually strong individuals may take as long as a hundred years.

From the intense attention required in practice and in two-person interaction, deep levels of sensitivity are learned. Seeing and feeling are not possible without sensitivity. The practitioner must be inwardly still and tranquil so that the noise of his own being does not obscure that which is coming from outside. This is achieved by letting go of the gross and anaesthetised sensibility of daily life, and opening up awareness to new territory.

Early in life, moral values are intact, but they are weakened through life by the pitfalls of society and by bad experiences. A healthy resistance to corrupting influences can help with a return to nature. Embrace a simple life by accepting and doing your best. Do not expect too much from others. If they fall short, accept their shortcomings with understanding. Strive for sincerity and nobility in your actions.

The Samurai practised Ju-jitsu in order to protect themselves and others when they were unable to use their swords. Today, Ju-jitsu continues to fill a need in Western society to combat stress and strengthen personal health and character. The art of Ju-jitsu is dedicated to those who wish to pursue a better way of life through the cultivation of the mind, body and spirit.

Even though the Jitsuka's path today is completely different from that of the warrior of the past, it is not necessary to abandon totally the old ways. Absorb venerable traditions and philosophy into this art by clothing them with fresh garments, and build on the classic principles to create modern forms.

Harmony and Balance in Training and Life

The philosophy of the martial arts is the achieving of harmonious values by individuals who live by peace, wisdom, morals, love and self-discipline through intellectual means. The martial arts philosophy consists of a basic paradox: magnificent amounts of energy are devoted towards learning how to fight, but the practitioner is supposed to avoid a fight at all costs. Even the name 'martial art' seems to be a contradiction.

The aim is to integrate fighting and philosophy, allowing participants to enjoy the satisfaction and enlightenment gained in competition with peers, as well as giving spectators a thrilling glimpse into a fascinating world. In order to achieve these goals the Ju-jitsu practitioner must always consider the philosophy of the art rather than just the physical aspects. He must conduct himself in an honourable and respectable manner according to traditional concepts of purity and truth, death and life, serenity and peace.

Ju-jitsu aims to achieve harmony with the offender, with other persons, with the environment, and with the practitioner's self; it is 'the spirit of loving protection for all beings'. Since the fundamental principle acquired through the practice of Ju-jitsu has been elevated to a finer moral concept of gentleness, softness and flexibility, it may well be said that the primary objective of practising Ju-jitsu is perfection of character.

Every individual has a distinct personality and role in life. It is possible to learn in isolation, but growing along with others in mutual respect leads to harmony.

Martial art comes down to the concept of balance – it is both 'martial' and 'art'. If it is too martial, it is mere thuggery; with too much art, the practitioner is fooling himself as to his ability. It is necessary to train hard, but safely – but not too safely. As a student you will always be walking along the edge of the sword, striving to learn under the conditions most closely approximating true danger, yet at the same time respecting your own physical well-being and the physical well-being of your classmates.

Ju-jitsu practitioners should try to achieve and maintain balance in their life, since balance is the cardinal principle of efficiency. This comprises an internal balance, which unifies the mind and body, as well as the actual physical balance of the body. Balance is a dynamic state, involving constant adjustment even when standing still. When the body is in a state of true balance, it is poised to move and work most efficiently. The mind and body have innate mechanisms that act to maintain the alignment and balance of the body, in motion and at rest.

Inner balance and harmony with others allow the individual to build values that lead to self-confidence. If there is a lack of self-control or balance within, it can have an effect on a person's attitude toward others. Modest students are aware and always ready to learn. Others will sense this, and respect will be gained. Arrogance, on the other hand, is a weakness, because it restricts learning ability. Having a non-defeatist attitude takes courage and sacrifice and leads to constant growth, even through difficulties and hardships. In order to have a full understanding of himself, the individual must explore the consequences of his actions (or potential actions) and decide what path he would take – before coming to the fork in the road.

Ju-jitsu is an art with which to master conflict by means of harmonizing with the life energy that animates the opponent and pervades nature. Through this all-embracing state of harmony, it is possible to overcome an opponent, or to face the tests of life, by arriving at a state of non-resistance. Jitsuka learn to manifest harmony by studying rigorous, effective self-defence techniques that are not passive but extremely dynamic. The study of Ju-jitsu can allow the student to respond quickly and flexibly to life's changes, without being overwhelmed by them.

The Five Sources of Power

The proper purpose of Ju-jitsu practice is training the body and cultivating the mind, to nurture the spirit, and contribute to the welfare flowing into the world. Ju-jitsu seeks to create such an environment in which the Jitsuka can work on all the aspects of life that they need to work on, in order to gain joyful inner peace and start the path of enlightenment.

In practice, this starts with the mastery of the physical being, the body. As the practitioner masters his physical body he has also started on the path of mastering his mind. Physical exercise is for the body, while meditation is the exercise for the mind.

The natural sequence of the five sources of power begins with the mind. Without the power of mind (yi), everything else is without source. When the mind is in proper perspective, power of the body (li) will have its opportunity to flourish. With the body growing strong, the spirit manifests itself in inspiring outward behaviour, which is easy to observe in anyone with great spirit. To affect the soul is a searching process that comes with time and repetition (wisdom), this is manifest in mature behaviour and understanding of others. The power of energy (qi) allows the individual to flow with energy from within his centre, and to share this energy with others.

Mind

The mind is a very important source of power. Even if an individual has a lot of body strength, any doubts about his ability will mean that he will have a hard time achieving his goal. A positive attitude will always help. The power of the mind is described in a number of terms, such as 'mind over matter' or 'accomplishing the goal by a force of will'.

Body

The body is an obvious source of power and strength, made stronger through body conditioning, weight training and stamina-oriented exercises. The Ju-jitsu practitioner should stay simple and pure and should not pollute his body with that which is unnatural. His body is as a sword. If he cares for it, it should remain strong and sharp; if it is neglected, it will break when needed most. Do not overindulge in luxury, because luxury over clouds the mind. Jitsuka should not use illegal drugs. Ju-jitsu is a drug-free martial art, and all Ju-jitsu practitioners are expected to be drug-free. Also they should not associate with, or be in the company of, others who use illegal drugs. The Jitsuka also should avoid alcohol abuse and tobacco dependency. For health think right, eat right, exercise right, rest right and perform right.

Spirit

'The power of a positive attitude' refers to one's spirit. If we approach things with enthusiasm and focus, we can accomplish many goals. We can also share our good spirit with others and better develop teamwork. Even when things are not going well, a strong spirit can help one overcome many obstacles.

Soul

The soul is the very private and personal essence of one's being. While the spirit is an outward expression of power and energy, the soul is an internal source of strength. Our ethics and system of principles lie within our soul, and by making decisions and facing challenges from your centre of good principles, we can feel confident that we are taking the best path for us. 'A kind heart' makes reference to that person's soul and inner being.

Energy

Qi (Pronounced 'key') is a Japanese word that refers to the invisible life force that flows freely throughout the world and the universe. The term describes the vital internal energy that animates all living things as well as all of nature. Qi is a basic concept in most martial arts and lies at the root of martial

and meditative arts practices. It is also known as prhana (India), chi (China) and ki (Japan), all words that generally translate into 'breath'.

Life is constituted by qi (in the sense of 'breath' and 'energy') – a force that manifests itself in respiration and can be felt circulating within the body. By concentrating and focusing on relaxing the body and 'flowing' the qi, it is possible to express power greater than 'normal' body strength. Qi represents the power of the mind in union with the body.

Qi is almost always perceived as a subtle force, produced by mental discipline, and is manifested in so-called 'internal arts'. Many martial artists believe in a distinction between internal and external (or soft/hard) styles. If an art is being performed by a living entity, it must contain an internal and an external component. If a qi-based art is seen as different from an external art, it is because the emphasis is on subtle techniques that use pressure points, deceptive approach and a disciplined gentleness in delivery.

When qi flows freely and without inhibition, the body has great power as a result of the five sources. In this status of shen, it can do wonderful things, but when qi ceases to flow, the body becomes dull and weak.

Qi is neither generated by characters nor destroyed by characters. Rather, characters channel qi. In this sense it flows through them and obeys their will. The stronger the characters, the more easily qi will obey them and the greater power it will give them.

Every Jitsuka should fortify his body, find his own way, flay his sprit, feed his soul and flow his qi.

Paths to Follow

Discipline in all three areas – body, mind and spirit – allows the individual to discover his own way of life. Determination and discipline must be his mental path. A healthy body and hard training must be his physical path. Daily training gives good health, balances the mind and body and, above all, brings about a positive and loving attitude towards life. Courage, love and caring must be the individual's spiritual path. Travelling those paths, you must strive always to seek the best. If you create a love for perfection, you will gain honour through honesty, loyalty, sincerity and pride. This will be not a possessive love, but an unconditional love.

A true martial artist must have knowledge of the philosophical, spiritual, artistic and physical world that surrounds him. The holistic approach of Ju-jitsu encompasses not only the mental and physical but also the spiritual self-development and moral aspects of total well-being. The true authentic philosophy of Ju-jitsu promotes peace and harmony by encouraging genuine love, care and protection of all things.

Knowing about Health

The martial arts set down the basis for human health, and health is the most important aspect of the arts. In order to maximize health, the individual must increase his knowledge of health.

Health relates to three realms: the physical, the mental and the spiritual. If he follows the discipline appropriately, a practitioner of the martial arts can develop happiness through attaining a healthy base in these three areas. The three areas are not independent of one another and each plays an important interactive role with the others. The right level of satisfaction and overall health can be achieved only by working in all three areas.

Physical Health
If a Ju-jitsu practitioner is physically fit, he will feel good about his health. This transforms into a general good feeling about life. Most major issues in a person's life can be subsumed under the premise of fear of death and dying. If a person is physically fit, then the prospect of death is more remote. The martial arts provide a structure, which is beneficial for physical well-being in two important ways:

1. It provides physical enhancement through the training that a Ju-jitsu practitioner receives in the dojo;
2. It provides a motivation to stay physically fit outside of the dojo, too.

The Ju-jitsu practitioner realizes that he must stay fit and respect his body outside of the dojo as well as inside. In other words, he must obey the rules of the martial arts as a lifestyle, not just in specific situations. Physical health goes beyond physical training and enters into physiology. When a person eats properly, he feels better and can further enhance his physical training. This is also set out in the rules of the martial arts. Proper nutrition means less consumption of foods and drinks that do not benefit health.

A safe learning environment is essential and a number of conditions pose a threat to a healthy martial arts environment. The importance of hygiene and cleanliness cannot be over-stated. Martial arts training requires close physical contact and a safe, clean, professional atmosphere is vital. Refined cleanliness means a refined mind. Clean clothes and a clean body show by example the honour and ethics held.

Mental Health
If a Ju-jitsu practitioner is mentally fit, he will feel good about his life. This will transform into a generally good attitude about the world and those in it. A person who does not like himself is likely to fail in relationships.

Being involved with the world provides for better mental health. The opposite approach provides a negative framework and allows for personality disorders.

If a Ju-jitsu practitioner gains a stronger mental health along with physical and spiritual health, he becomes healthy in a well-rounded way. For example, if an individual puts too much emphasis on being physically fit, his mental health may suffer. He may have problems in his relationships if his focus is only physical. Furthermore, if his mental health is poor as a result, he will not be able to assist the physical aspects in compensating for inevitable issues such as age, muscular breakdown, and so on. Having only physical health also provides for detachment and a poor sense of self. This is why it is important to ensure that a Ju-jitsu practitioner works on all three areas.

Spiritual Health

If a Ju-jitsu practitioner is spiritually fit, he will feel good about his sense of being. The physical and mental parts are irrelevant unless there is a sense of being a part of something 'bigger'. This does not necessarily relate to religion. Religion is spiritual to some, but others who are spiritual are not necessarily religious. Without a sense of being, he cannot belong.

The Ju-jitsu art helps practitioners with a sense of belonging and hence their spiritual side that assists with their sense of being.

Energy, breathing, movement and mental attitude, as well as interaction and balance between them, are indivisible elements necessary for improvement of physical and mental health.

4 Getting Started and the Dojo

Choosing the Right Club

Club Facilities

According to an old saying, 'When the pupil is ready, the Master will appear.' To help this happen you need know what you are looking for and should be selective when looking for a club. There may only be one club in your area, but the following checklist should help you make the right decision.

- Location – is the club in a neighborhood where you and your child feel safe? If you are not sure, consider asking at the local police station.
- Is the club clean? Well-maintained toilets are always a good sign.
- Are the students scruffy? Their personal presentation is a reflection on their instructor.
- Some facilities have good dressing rooms and lockers while others provide only an extra room to change in. Are you comfortable with these arrangements? Does any one else have access to the room during training?
- In the actual training area, or dojo, as it is commonly known, are the mats in good condition? Are they the plastic-covered type or the old canvas ones? The plastic ones can be cleaned at the end of each session whereas the canvas ones harbour years of dead skin, bloodstains and nasty bacteria!
- Is there a good safety area around the perimeter, or will you be rolling or falling against radiators or other furniture?
- Is the other equipment, including punch bags, in good condition?

Instructor/Teacher/Coach

The Ju-jitsu instructor is usually addressed as Sensei (pronounced 'Sen say').

Observe the coach or instructor in action. Does he make himself understood to the students? Does he support the students? Does he criticize and make fun of them? Is he willing to explain and answer any questions? Does he give feedback at the end of the session? The instructor should get involved and interact with other members of the student's family who may be waiting at the end of the class.

Instructors become role models and all instructors should remind themselves of the saying, 'Attitudes are contagious. Is yours worth catching?'

Do not be afraid to ask to see the instructor's qualifications. He should be pleased and proud to show you them. You should also ask for the phone number of the national governing body, to ensure that the club is registered and that all students are fully insured.

A bit of knowledge about the instructor's background is vital. Ask the instructor how long he has been teaching Ju-jitsu, who teaches him, and whether he continues his development by attending courses, and so on. An instructor's teachers will have passed on to him many of their ideas and training methods, including the philosophy, ethics and structure of the club. All good coaches need to keep themselves updated with the latest training, coaching and exercise programmes. Some expect their students simply to accept them as a role model and to emulate them, and lead the way in all aspects of training within the club; some believe that there is no need to have an interest in the history of their art, encouraging their students to get on and train; others will insist on an understanding of the philosophies of the art and its roots. Every student needs to decide which type is the most suitable instructor for him.

Be wary of an instructor who teaches all martial arts. It takes a lifetime to study properly one discipline, or maybe two at the most.

Club Development

After carrying out the basic checks, you are in a position to make a more discerning and objective appraisal of a club and its instructors.

Ask about your potential for growth within the club and in the wider view of the Ju-jitsu world in general. Does the club have specialist classes that cater for different grades? In those clubs that have a special night for the instructors to train under the chief instructor, there is always good pupil progress.

How successful is the club in terms of recruiting and keeping students right through their grades? Does the club have opportunities for competition (see Chapter 11 for more on this aspect of the art)?

Ask if the club is run on a professional basis and whether the instructor is a full-time Ju-jitsu practitioner. It may be that the club is run on a committee basis, in which case you might want to ask to see a copy of the constitution.

Grades

Ask about the grading structure and how many belts are in the system. It is a good idea to know approximately how long you need to train for each belt. The instructor is usually the coordinator of the club's teaching programme.

Grading structures allow students to see how they are progressing. A number of clubs now use other methods such as attendance badges and various skill badges, which are an intermediate way of showing that the student is progressing and learning the required skills needed for the next grading. If you are interested in competitions, ask to view the medals and trophies that the club has won.

Children in Ju-Jitsu

General Benefits

Children really enjoy the experience of learning new skills and Ju-jitsu is ideal for them. Different schools have different philosophies. Seek out a school that teaches physical skills that will give your child a feeling of self-confidence. Some have programmes that teach children how to cope intelligently with the problem of bullying. The teacher and the school should embrace the positive values of dignity, respect, humility and honesty.

Ju-jitsu will help the child to treat others with respect and to get along with other people. This can be done with the use of storytelling and role play, both of which will stretch the child's imagination. Children will discover through Ju-jitsu that it is possible to resolve conflict peacefully, and that there are alternatives to violence. Children will also learn self-control and soon come to understand that everyone benefits from cooperation. Even in competition it is possible to bring out the best of these ethics and to teach children to be strong and confident. During both training and competition, they can be taught to channel their aggression, in a safe environment.

Group listening to a 'positive' martial arts story.

Children should learn Ju-jitsu piece by piece and will progress by being rewarded every time they learn something new, or accomplish a set goal.

In the photos opposite, two 14-year-olds are working together to develop some reasonably advanced techniques. This is building and expanding their comfort zone, and further developing hand/eye coordination. They have also learnt that they need to cooperate with each other in order to obtain the best results.

Application of locks on young, growing joints needs to be meticulously supervised. Young joints have growing spaces and these can easily be damaged by overzealous application of technique.

Teaching Children

Control at all levels of Ju-jitsu is paramount. As a child begins to understand the under-lying principles of the philosophy of Ju-jitsu, he will become more successful in other aspects of life. Success comes from choosing the path in life that is inspirational. Ju-jitsu school training programmes should be exciting and unique. They should create a positive attitude, offer exciting goals, give improved confidence, improved responsibility and persistence to allow for success in life.

It should be the goal of every Ju-jitsu instructor to give every child the essential tools to be his or her best. These tools include the self-esteem to stand tall, the persistence never to quit, the discipline to stay on track and the imagination to make dreams a reality. The gift of self-esteem empowers children to achieve in all areas of their life, at school and at home, in sports as well as in the community. Ju-jitsu training should always be structured to bring out the best in a child.

Practising a figure four lock.

Stopping a throw halfway to make sure position is correct.

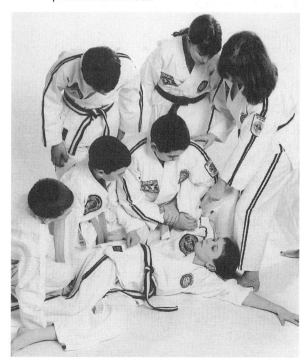

Group session reinforcing the points that the teacher is pointing out.

Fun, happiness, and achieving goals, are the cornerstones of good classes.

Many clubs now incorporate games, based on balance, stamina, concentration, speed, endurance, as a way of teaching and learning in a fun environment that is particularly suitable for children. Other clubs may emphasize the more rigid traditional methods. A good club would probably incorporate both.

Physical Benefits

Historically, children have always started early in their study of Ju-jitsu and, indeed, in most other martial arts.

Children who take up Ju-jitsu enjoy numerous physical benefits. Their flexibility, reflexes, agility and coordination all improve greatly and this has the bonus of making them better at other physical activities in which they may be involved. The benefits of general exercise are indisputable, and the specific exercises of Ju-jitsu training develop quick reflexes, muscular strength, flexibility, coordination and good hand/eye skills. Exercise builds strong bones, helps prevent heart disease, improves cardiovascular fitness and, in many cases, helps to reduce high blood pressure and decrease depression.

The physical training that is required for the practice of Ju-jitsu decreases hostility, emphasizing the defence aspect of the art and not the attack. Sleep patterns are improved. Hyperactivity in many cases is reduced and the ability to concentrate on other subjects is another bonus.

The aerobic-type activity at the beginning

of each Ju-jitsu class is particularly beneficial for cardiovascular fitness.

Children must learn to breathe properly, particularly since the majority of adults use only about one-third of the capacity of their lungs. The lack of expansion in the chest and abdominal cavity means that oxygen is not delivered to all parts of the body as it should be. Many children's problems such as asthma and glue ear benefit from proper breathing.

Children tend to develop muscular strength that is not necessarily in proportion to their size. Although strength is important, Ju-jitsu does not demand muscular superiority. Technique and the skill of the practitioner is much more important, yet strength is increased by the exercises required. Proportionate development is witnessed as the children progress through the years.

Most children are naturally quite flexible, and maintaining flexibility is the key to enjoying Ju-jitsu into adult life.

Children have growing spaces between their joints and great care should be taken that these are preserved and protected by doing safe, appropriate exercise.

Discomfort with their ever-changing bodies can make some children seem ungainly. It is at this stage that they need as much confidence-boosting as possible and a good teacher will make sure that this happens. Handing out praise is very important.

Children learn and pick up skills at different levels of development. A good teacher will ensure that the lesson embraces all these stages.

Exercises and Games for Children

Classes should embrace a balanced approach of play combined with discipline.

For the reflexes: the teacher holds a pile of magazines (with edges taped, to make them more stable) up in front of a line of students. Each student stands ready to throw a punch at a magazine that is dropped by the teacher in front of him. As their reactions speed up, the more direct hits the students score. The same exercise can be used for the development of blocking skills.

'Crocodile' is another great reflex exercise. The teacher takes two pieces of plastic tube covered in foam, to represent the crocodile's mouth. He stands in front of the children, holding the foam tubes at each end and opening and closing them like a mouth. The children take turns to punch through the space between the 'jaws', while the teacher tries to snap the jaws shut on their arm. This can be used in conjunction with kicking skills.

The Bubble Game should only be played on a floor that can be wiped over afterwards. The children are put into teams and the teams are assigned to different areas on the mat. (This is for safety as they can become over-enthusiastic and the class can be chaotic.) The bubble machine is set going and, as the bubbles drift down to their level, the children have to practise their blocking, kicking and punching skills to pop them before they hit the floor.

The Noise Game is good for enhancing the listening, reaction and coordination skills of students. The teacher brings a variety of noise makers – whistle, bell, buzzer, drum, squeaker, and so on – to the class, and tells the students that each noise represents a certain technique, such as a throw or a kick. When they hear the specific noise, they have to react to it as quickly as possible by performing the technique. This game can be played with elimination in each round, ending up with one winner. The noises can also be changed around, requiring them to to concentrate even harder.

Women in Ju-Jitsu

Self-defence is usually the main reason why

women take up Ju-jitsu and it is very effective in this respect. There are certain challenges to be met by women in an arena that has traditionally been male-dominated, but the discipline really is for everyone. There is a certain amount of negativity towards women in the martial arts, but this usually as a result of men's misconceptions, and most schools will discourage unequal treatment of women. Many women find that they can fit in easily, but this depends greatly on the school chosen.

There are a number of issues relating to menstruation and pregnancy, but a school or club that has a good success rate in the development of female students will certainly be able to give the right advice.

Bodily contact when working with a partner, whether male or female, can be a challenging obstacle, but most practitioners overcome it without too much fuss.

The numbers of women taking up Ju-jitsu is increasing and there are now some very high-ranking female exponents, some of whom have been training and teaching for over twenty-five years. And much further back than this, there are many historical references to women in the martial arts. In Japan, women were often extremely skilled in the art of Tanto Jutsu, which was developed from the throwing of a knife or dagger. The women carried the knife around with them at all times and it became their equivalent of the sword that men would carry. Japanese chronicles include many stories of the exploits of warrior queens leading troops into battle. Some Samurai women were trained to be as loyal and as totally commit-

Defending against a strangle by striking under the jaw with the elbow.

Defending against a strangle from behind by striking to the solar plexus with the elbow.

ted as their fathers, brothers and husbands. This female warrior class were dominant in their military roles and possessed great skill and strength, with and without weapons. Today, women continue to excel in the use of naginata, a traditional weapon, which is still taught in many Ju-jitsu schools in an aesthetic form of kata.

The Dojo

Respect and courtesy for your fellow student are the foundation of all martial arts. Check before you leave home that your gi (training uniform) is clean and pressed. Cut your fingernails and toenails and take a shower. No one wants to train with someone whose personal hygiene is not up to scratch. Arrive early at the dojo to give yourself time to change and chat with your fellow students. Remove all jewellery and tie long hair back. Bow when you enter the dojo or training area. Slippers (zoris) are worn and then removed when stepping on to the training mat (tatami).

It is important to follow the correct procedures when embarking upon any field of activity. Ju-jitsu is no different. Because it encompasses many varied movements, correct preparation for the rigours of training is essential.

Dojo Etiquette

The practitioner must be guided constantly by a deep respect for the dojo, for all the people in it, and for the purpose of the practice. Good manners, politeness, courteous behaviour, and maintenance of formal etiquette are part of a practitioner's training, and essential to developing a respectful attitude to the art. The practitioner should memorize the rules, and always obey them.

There are several basic rules relating to conduct in the dojo.

Learning to use the naginata.

The Bow
If standing, bend forward at the waist. Retain eye contact with the person to whom you are bowing. If kneeling, place your hands flat on the floor in front of you so that your hands are touching or overlapping. Touch your forehead to your hands.

When a higher Black Belt member enters a studio with a class in session the coach will stop the class, and acknowledge his presence by having the class bow to him.

Entering/Exiting the Dojo
No practitioner should join or leave class in progress without the permission of the coach. Face the room and bow as you enter or exit the dojo.

Working with a Partner

Show respect by bowing to your partner both before and after working together.

Sitting Seiza

Seiza ('correct, calm sitting') is a kneeling posture associated with Japanese meditative forms. Whenever sitting in class, sit seiza or with your legs crossed. Never sit with your legs outstretched.

Stepping On/Off the Mat

Always takes off your shoes before you step on the mat. Only approved shoes are to be worn on the mat. Face the centre of the mat and bow before you step on or off the mat. Step on with the left foot; step off with the right foot.

Start/Close of Class

Line up, sitting seiza, facing tatami or the practising area. Practitioners will sit in sequence, depending on rank. When you hear shomen-ni, bow to the front of the class. When you hear sensei-ni, bow to the class. For the close of class you will line up the same, but the bows are in reverse order.

As a sign of respect for their elders, students remain in seiza after the class has ended, until all the higher-ranking dojo buddies have bowed off the mat. No practitioner should join or leave a class in progress without the coach's permission.

Joining/ Leaving Classes in Progress

In order to join a class in progress, stand at the edge of the mat and wait for the coach to bow you on. When you must leave before the class is concluded, tell the coach you wish to bow off before leaving the mat. Whenever you leave the mat (regardless of the reason or expected duration), stand at the edge of the mat and make eye contact with the coach. Wait for the coach to bow to you before leaving the mat.

Written Guidelines

Many Ju-jitsu clubs are run on the basis that a new student will gradually pick things up as he goes along, but it is much more constructive and useful to give every student a set of guidelines at the beginning.

Ju-jitsu places a great emphasis on the development of the character through the development of the body. Using a code of behaviour together with the physical training means that technical skill, physical fitness and good behaviour become synonymous with the art.

The code is based on a mutual respect between teachers and students, and respect for seniority. Practitioners are expected also to show respect for the society in which they live, and for others who live in and administer that society. All Ju-jitsu associations should aim to produce high-quality teachers, students and competitors. Students have a duty to behave in a way that will enhance and maintain the reputation of their club. The instructors have a particular responsibility, as they will greatly influence the behaviour of their students both inside and outside the dojo. Bad behaviour on the part of an instructor will reflect badly on the association's chief instructor. Instructors should ensure that all students follow the club's code of behaviour.

Code of Behaviour

A code of behaviour hand-out for new students to the dojo might resemble the example shown opposite.

Competition Etiquette

The competition arena should be treated in the same way as the dojo, with the same respect shown to seniors and to all others involved. Competition is sometimes seen as glamorous, and competitors, especially those who become successful, will become 'role models' and can have a marked

Rules and Regulations of Conduct for use inside the Dojo

- Always bow on entering or leaving the dojo.
- Junior grades must bow first to their seniors.
- Instructors should be referred to as Sensei or by their appropriate title and not their name.
- Nails must be kept clean and short enough to avoid scratching or cutting.
- Jewellery and watches should not be worn. If it is not possible to remove rings or earrings, they should be safely covered. It may be requested that shoes are removed when entering the dojo.
- Mobile phones should be switched off unless the student is on emergency call-out, in which case he should inform the instructor.
- Classes will start with a bow to your Sensei and to other students. This is a greeting and a sign of respect. Sensei's instructions must be followed to the letter at all times. Unruly students are a danger to themselves and to others.
- Late arrivals should enter the dojo quietly, change and warm up in the changing room. When they wish to join the class, they must kneel to the front and side of the class, where they can be clearly seen by the Sensei, and watch carefully for the Sensei's signal to join in. When the signal is given, they should remain kneeling, bow deeply, then walk quickly and quietly around the back of the class until it is convenient to go to a position appropriate to their grade.
- Smoking is not allowed in the dojo, nor in any adjacent areas.
- Any behaviour that is likely to offend the etiquette of the dojo is not allowed.
- The individual student has a responsibility to see that his gi fits correctly and is kept clean and in a good state of repair. Tears and other damage must be repaired prior to the next training session. Association and club badges should be embroidered or stitched on to the gi. The belt of appropriate colour, including any necessary stripes or tabs, should be worn with the gi at all times.
- Ju-jitsu students have a responsibility to behave in a manner that enhances and maintains the reputation of the club and of their chosen art, both inside and outside the dojo. Students should not engage in 'impetuous and violent behaviour'.

influence on the behaviour of others, particularly young and immature students. Successful competitors must exhibit exemplary behaviour with regard to dress, sportsmanship and general behaviour, both on and off the competition area. This encompasses matters such as general deportment – not lounging around, for example – and showing respect for other competitors, officials and spectators.

Referees and judges must also show exemplary behaviour in the above matters.

5 Exercise and Injury

Ju-Jitsu and Fitness

Ju-jitsu is an excellent way of keeping fit, encompassing all the main attributes of fitness:

- agility;
- flexibility;
- power;
- reflexes;
- coordination;
- speed; and
- endurance.

Age is no barrier to exercise and its benefits. The more a person exercises, the better his chances of outliving his peers, as exercise seems to reduce the effects of ageing. Regular aerobic exercise not only helps to preserve neurological functioning into old age, but may also enhance it in formerly sedentary older people. Staying physically active appears to be increasingly important as a person ages. Incorporating a relatively modest amount of activity in what was once a sedentary lifestyle leads to the greatest surge in life expectancy.

The problems of ageing, such as increased body fat, decreased muscular strength and flexibility, loss of bone mass, lower metabolism and slower reaction times, can be minimized by exercise. In order to get benefits from any form of exercise, it must become a long-term habit, and Ju-jitsu is certainly that.

Ju-jitsu can also help with weight loss and weight maintenance by building muscle tissue. The only exercise that burns fat is aerobic exercise and Ju-jitsu is aerobic. Variety in Ju-jitsu training is one of the keys to staying fit. Cross-training allows more muscle groups to be exercised than a single activity, and variety also keeps Ju-jitsu classes from becoming monotonous.

Exercise safely

All exercises should be carried out with caution and according to current guidelines. There are a number of excellent resources available today to help the teacher and student to deliver the most appropriate exercises for the activity of Ju-jitsu.

Prevention of Injuries

Warming Up

Instructors have a responsibility to be aware of current good practice, particularly in the area of safety. Good health and fitness are often high on the list of members' reasons for joining a Ju-jitsu club. Students often seek advice from their instructor with regard to their general health, or with regard to supplementary exercises to help with their Ju-jitsu fitness, and instructors should have a general understanding of the fundamentals of body maintenance and development. They should ensure that any advice is given responsibly, is within their range of knowledge, and is safe and in the best interest of the student.

The best advice is to do exercises recommended as being safe and beneficial by your senior instructors. There are many sources of advice on physiology, and although well intentioned, not all are appropriate. If in doubt, check with a senior instructor.

Warming up involves raising the heart rate with light aerobic-type exercise, such as jogging. This raises the body temperature and increases the blood supply to muscles, allowing safer stretching, with less risk of injury. There is also a psychological purpose for warming up – it brings the class together to a state of mental and emotional readiness, regardless of the separate activities in which they were engaged prior to joining the training session.

The necessary warm-up and preparation time can vary greatly from person to person and from situation to situation. Experienced practitioners may develop their own routine with which they are comfortable and which is perfectly safe. They may need to pay more attention to a particular part of the warm-up or to a particular part of the body, and with experience and common sense this will be safe and acceptable. Many experienced practitioners of Ju-jitsu combine the warm-up and stretch by doing Ju-jitsu movements in a light and careful way, for example, performing one or more kata with gentle and stretched-out techniques. However, a structured warm-up and stretch routine should also prepare students mentally for Ju-jitsu training.

The term 'warm-up' is often used to describe the activity that takes place prior to actual Ju-jitsu training. Here, the term describes specifically the process of increasing the blood circulation prior to stretching. Sustained light exercise increases the blood flow to the working muscles and surrounding areas – an increased blood supply brings more heat, which makes the muscles soft and more elastic, and therefore less prone to injury. It also brings more oxygen and nutrients, and switches the metabolism to a more efficient system of generating the amount of energy that is required for a period of intense and dynamic activity.

In anatomical terms, a warm-up involves the use of the major muscles to pump a faster supply of blood to all the skeletal muscles and organs, giving them sufficient blood to allow them to function. A violent change in the workload can catch the system unprepared, resulting in a much greater potential for injury and much less efficiency.

In practice, a warm-up should consist of gentle and sustained working of muscles. A gentle jog around the dojo for three to four minutes is fine, as is gently bouncing on the spot. Both use the calf muscles as the main 'pump', but the shoulders and arms and many other muscles will also come in to play. Such exercises are referred to as 'aerobic', because they demand oxygen for the blood.

At this stage, movements must be gentle and controlled, not violent.

An alternative to aerobic exercise might be the simple act of moving the body into different positions, especially if this involves moving to and from the floor. This will eventually warm the body, but it will take longer and may not be sufficient if the dojo is not warm enough. If it is particularly cold, it might be necessary to 'top up' the warm-up, perhaps midway through the session, and at the end of stretching.

Stretching and Mobility Exercises
Stretched muscles and mobile joints are not only less likely to suffer injury, but are also capable of greater reach and speed.

Stretching should be progressive and involve all the major muscle groups. The instructor should not demonstrate ballistic (bouncing or jerking) movements in the early phase of stretching. The best results are obtained when a muscle is stretched to a degree where it feels uncomfortable but not painful. This stretch should be held for about ten seconds, and then the muscle should be relaxed. This process should be repeated three to four times. If the stretch does become too painful, the muscle will tighten to resist over-stretching and damage, and the process becomes self-defeating.

An alternative process is to use a technique known as PNF. In this process, the same uncomfortable stretch position should be reached, but then the stretched muscle should be firmly tensed for about 6 seconds. Immediately the muscle is relaxed, it will be possible to move deeper into the stretch.

It is best to stretch the muscles a little every day and comprehensively two to three times a week.

An instructor should watch to see that students do not modify an exercise in such a way that it becomes less effective or unsafe. Particular attention should be paid to any modification of exercises affecting the joints. Joints should be exercised in their natural alignment. Movements that stretch ligaments and weaken joints, such as knee twists or hyper-extension, should be avoided. However, the more fit and strong members, who have built up strong muscle around their joints, can perform more demanding stretching exercises.

The neck should be exercised in its natural plane of movement – neck rolls are not advised, especially at speed. Movements where the body is involved in unsupported leaning are not recommended. For example, leaning backwards in an unsupported way causes hyper-extension of the spine and vastly increases the risk of injury.

Care in Ju-Jitsu Training

The warm-up and stretch should have prepared the body for the dynamic and ballistic nature of Ju-jitsu movements. The instructor needs to know how to teach techniques in a manner that will not inflict injury on the practitioner, either in the short or the long term, and this demands an understanding of the physiology involved. Damage could result from 'bouncing' off a joint, or by creating excessive momentum against a natural alignment, for example, by not pivoting the supporting foot during certain kicks.

Strengthening exercises for the arms, legs and trunk, and aerobic and anaerobic conditioning should be done in line with current good practice. Care should always be taken, for example, when performing sit-ups – the knees should be bent and the base of the spine should be kept in contact with the floor, with a slight tilting of the pelvis.

Warm-Down

It is important to warm down at the end of strenuous exercise. It is much better for the cardiovascular system to ease off slowly, and this also helps to dissipate the lactic acid from joints, reducing stiffness and soreness. In practice, this means a few minutes of light activity, using a selection of activities from the warm-up and stretches.

Rest and Diet

Rest is important, and over-training or lack of sleep can lead to physiological stress. A recent study on the diet of athletes concluded that, except for endurance sports such as marathons, no special diet was required, but rather a proportional increase in quantity of a balanced diet. Ju-jitsu is physically very demanding, and it is necessary to prepare the body properly in order to prevent injury and to maximize performance.

Injuries

Emergency Situations

A Ju-jitsu instructor should be a qualified first aider and should encourage students to follow first aid courses too. In the event of an emergency or accident, the instructor will be expected to take charge, and he should have a detailed knowledge of emergency procedures.

When a student first attends a class he should be made aware of the location of fire exits and of evacuation procedures. It is the instructor's job to be able to account for all students at all times, and for this reason every student should register at the beginning of each class.

The following points need to be considered by the instructor when dealing with emergencies:

- Keep calm, take charge of the situation, organize immediate help.
- Deal promptly with any potentially life-threatening situation.
- Give reassurance to any injured party.
- Be aware that people may be affected by shock.
- Hospital treatment may be required, so no drugs, food or drinks should be given.

Accident prevention is always the first priority, but in the event of an accident the instructor should be able to care for any injured person without causing further complications. He should also be able to recognize when it is necessary to call an ambulance. The instructor should always know how to get to the nearest hospital and be able to arrange transportation if required. He should also know the location of the nearest telephone and have change or a phone card.

The instructor should be familiar with what is known as 'Emergency Aid' procedure and have the ability to deal quickly and confidently with life-threatening situations – for example, choking, cardiac arrest and severe bleeding. This proficiency can be gained by attending a recognized first aid course or by inviting a first aid instructor to the dojo. Proficiency requires practice and first aiders should attend appropriate refresher courses.

The club should have to hand contact numbers for all students and for all relevant authorities, in case of emergency. The keeping of a club accident book is highly recommended.

All clubs should have a well-stocked first aid box, which should be regularly replenished. Many clubs rely on the facility where the club trains to provide a first aid box, but the instructor should also have a portable one. The first aid box should be clearly marked and easily accessible, and should contain at least the following:

- Cotton bandages of various sizes;
- Triangular bandages;
- Crêpe bandages;
- Plasters;
- Safety pins;
- Sterilized gauze;
- Cotton wool;
- Scissors;
- Disposable gloves; and
- Disposable resuscitation gauze.

Basic Anatomy

The instructor should have a basic understanding of human anatomy and the functioning of the skeletal and muscular systems: the skeleton forms the rigid framework of the body; the periosteum is a layer of dense connective tissue that covers the surface of the bone, except at the articular surfaces; the outer layer of the periosteum is extremely dense and contains a large number of blood vessels; the inner layer is more cellular and contains fewer blood vessels; the periosteum provides attachment for the tendons and ligaments. Where two or more bones are connected, the joint has a capsule of fibrous tissue surrounding it. The ligaments link the two bones together at the joint. Capsules and ligaments are not very flexible and represent common sites for injury.

The major purpose of the muscles is to produce movements of the body. Muscles have a far greater blood supply than tendons and therefore heal much more quickly.

The bursa is a little fluid-filled sack of fibrous tissue, normally formed around joints and in places where ligaments and tendons pass over bones. Inflammation of the bursa produces pain and tenderness and, sometimes, restriction of the joint.

Nerves transmit impulses from the brain or spinal cord to the muscles.

Blood vessels are tubes carrying blood away from or towards the heart and the means by which the blood circulates through the body. They carry nutrients to the muscles, and take toxins away from them.

Common Injuries in Martial Arts

The most common injuries in martial arts are soft-tissue injuries. Strains, sprains and bruises can happen in Ju-jitsu training to even the most fit and flexible person, and they may have a serious effect on the soft tissues of the body. Soft-tissue injuries involve mainly the joint capsules, ligaments, muscles and tendons. It is important to treat soft-tissue injuries immediately and effectively.

These injuries can be divided into traumatic injuries and over-use injuries. A traumatic injury is usually caused by a sudden traumatic fall, landing on a joint, causing an overstretching of the soft tissues; a strain of the arm muscle when punching a focus pad; or perhaps a ballistic movement of the muscle and joint when missing a target.

A strain is an injury to muscles or tendons, whereas a sprain is an injury involving the joint capsules or ligaments. If blood vessels are damaged this will be made apparent by bruising.

RSI (Repetitive Strain Injury)

This type of injury occurs frequently in industry, when people have to stand or sit for hours a time, or carry out repetitive jobs, such as lifting without any variation of position, typing, or screwing with a screwdriver for long periods. Such injuries are very rare in Ju-jitsu but care should always be taken to increase levels of fitness and flexibility, and not to deviate from the technique being taught. Any equipment, including training surfaces, should be up to standard and suitable for the specific purpose for which it is being used.

Dealing with Injury

Every individual responds differently to injury, depending on the type of injury, the severity, the age of the person, the timescale from injury to commencement of treatment, the individual recovery rate and the treatment itself. Most injuries follow a pattern of soft-tissue damage followed by inflammation followed by repair.

If you are unfortunate enough to suffer this type of injury, the first step is to treat the inflammation with ice. Seek advice from your instructor and then expert advice from an osteopath, chiropractor or physiotherapist. Usually, after one visit and the right advice in the early stages, you will experience a speedy recovery and soon be able to return to full training.

6 Basic Development of Ju-Jitsu Techniques

Breakfalling

Ju-jitsu is rather like learning to walk all over again. You will be asked to adopt some peculiar stances, for example, but as you progress these will become quite natural. Your confidence will also be built up by learning how to break your fall (breakfalling).

There are four types of breakfall in Ju-jitsu: front, back, side, rolling and fore flap. It is vital to remember to breathe out when performing all breakfalls.

Breakfalling is designed so that, if you are thrown, you will be less likely to suffer injury. During training, you will soon learn how to breakfall and become very competent. You can be thrown to the ground at speeds of up to about 50 mph, so it is important to know how to land or fall correctly. The essence of breakfalling is demonstrated by the fact that, when being thrown on your side, you strike the mat with your arm at 45 degrees a split second before your body does. This may sting a little at first but the

Front breakfall.

Back breakfall.

arm is taking the shock of the fall.

The front breakfall is designed to allow you to fall or be pushed forward, landing on your forearms, while keeping your abdomen and face off the ground, thus avoiding injury.

The back breakfall allows you to fall or be pushed or thrown backward. Keep your chin on your chest, teeth together and tongue in the middle of your mouth. This will safeguard you from whiplash, banging the back of your head or biting your tongue. Throw both arms out to the side of your body at a 45-degree angle, with palms down, and strike the mat. The harder you can strike the mat, the more efficient your breakfall will be.

The side breakfall helps you to avoid injury while you are being pushed or thrown from the side. Start at a low level (for exam-ple, squatting) and allow your left leg to rise up and to the side. As you overbalance, your left arm should reach out and strike the mat. Avoid landing on your elbow. Repeat the process using your right leg and right arm.

The rolling breakfall is similar to the forward roll that everyone did as a child, but it must be done in a way that protects the spine from injury. Start off in a controlled manner and at a low level. Push off with your back leg and roll, first over your left side and then over your right. This simulates being thrown from the left and the right. As you progress, you will be able to do this from a running start, and roll without touching your hands on the mat. You should then be able to come straight back to your feet, facing the direction from which you have just

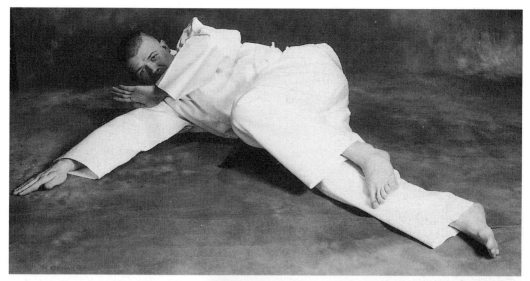

(*Above and right*) Side breakfall.

Rolling breakfall start and finish.

come and immediately adopting a defensive stance (see below).

To practise the fore flap breakfall, start by doing an assisted hand stand and then pull your arms away, landing on your back and slapping the mat with your arms at a 45-

Standard defensive stance.

Fore flap breakfall.

degree angle. Keep your spine off the mat, placing the emphasis on your shoulder girdle.

Stances

Stances allow you to be in a balanced defensive position and yet able to move fluidly into other moves and throws. Development of good stances and the ability to move from one stance into another are vital in Ju-jitsu. Balance and co-ordination are the foundations of good stances.

Why do the stances vary? Certainly, it is true that the needs of the fighting Samurai were very different from the needs of the martial arts practitioner today. Their clothes were different, as was the clothing of their adversary. They were defending against and attacking with weapons. Despite the differences, however, the principles of the stances have not changed much. Some of the stances themselves have hardly changed at all from the past, while others have changed a great deal. The need for a good strong defensive stance, which allows the body to move freely, is required just as much today as in the past. A low centre of gravity and equal spread of weight remain priorities.

Stances in sporting martial arts, and in Ju-jitsu, are different in that they need to allow the practitioner to score points quickly, with a controlled strike or kick. Being able to run in and take hold of the opponent requires a different, less rigid stance. Whatever the needs of the stance, the principles never change, and the most important thing is always to be aware of balance, posture and surroundings. After a period of expert training in the movements of Ju-jitsu, speed and accuracy should allow you to deal with any threatening situation or attack, but the traditional training in and understanding of the stances are none the less vital.

The standard stance (see the photo on page 45) is taught at beginner level to instill discipline of movement when performing punches and kicks. The back leg should be locked and the front knee bent. The feet should be shoulder width apart. The right hand should be held in a clenched fist while the left arm acts as a guard. Fingers should be slightly bent and together. The arm should also be slightly bent and in a position across the chest.

Other stances are the fighting stance, the horse stance and the cat stance. Fighting stance is a guarded posture against imminent attack. Bring the front leg back from defensive stance (see the photo on next page) ready to kick. For the back stance, the practitioner steps back from defensive stance (see the photo on page 49) in order to avoid a kick. Horse stance is used to deal with attacks from the side and looks as you would when astride a horse, though without the actual horse.

Fighting stance.

Horse stance.

Cat stance, bringing the front leg back from defensive Stance ready to kick.

Blocking

The ability to block an opponent's punch or kick is vital for defence, but merely blocking an opponent's attacks leads only to more attacks. The Ju-jitsu practitioner must develop the skill and ability to turn a block into a countering force, which becomes an integral part of a Ju-jitsu move. The ability to do this is a sure sign of a good Ju-jitsu exponent.

As you progress you will perform low-level simulated attacks and defences using many varied blocks and parries. You will develop the ability to move, twist and turn while remaining in control of your body and judging the distance between you and your attacker. Developing this ability takes time and effort, but 'the more you train the more you gain'.

Using Blocks

Blocking means defending an area of your body that is being attacked by using one or more of your limbs. In training, big gloves may be used to guard your body as your outer arms take hits, but there is no such protective equipment in the real world. Serious injury can occur to your limbs if you rely solely on this type of blocking. Sometimes, it will be impossible to use anything other than this method. For example, if you have been knocked to the ground and there is more than one attacker, it is absolutely essential to cover the vital areas of

Back stance.

your head and body. Broken limbs usually repair very well, but brain or vital organ damage is much more serious. As your training progresses you will automatically block and counter against attacks and you should be able to escape from such a situation without serious injury.

There are many varied techniques of blocking in the art of Ju-jitsu. Some involve parrying or deflecting, while others involve capturing. Ju-jitsu means 'the soft or pliable way', and the aim is to use the opponent's force to advantage, rather than meet attacks head on with brute force. Many of the Westernized forms of blocking in the martial arts have lost the true meaning of the art, and it is only in the last decade that a better

understanding of the more traditional 'blocks' has begun to emerge, and these blocks have begun to be taught.

The principle in almost all the techniques in Ju-jitsu is the fact that the actual defence is the combination of the block and the countering attack all rolled into one continuous move. For example, the Ju-jitsuka (another term for Jitsuka) will defend against a kick and, as he avoids it by deflection or capture, the next move of twisting, pulling, dislocating or breaking is already intertwined within the whole movement. The Ju-jitsuka needs to have a sound knowledge of nerve distribution and acupuncture points. These can be struck to devastating effect, causing the opponent to be in severe pain, immobile or unconscious. In the worst scenario, it is possible even to maim or kill, and this is why the teacher will not hand the knowledge down to students until they are ready and mature enough to understand it.

There are other potential dangers in blocking. For example, in blocking an attack such as a lapel grab, it is very easy to break the attacker's arm. The attacker takes tight hold of your lapel with his left hand, either to threaten or because he is going to throw a punch at you with his free hand. Reading the attack, you reach out in front of you and pretend you are taking hold of his jacket directly opposite your own arm, in other words, on the attacker's right side. If the attacker turns rapidly in a circle-like movement in an anti-clockwise direction and at the same time grabs your hand, not allowing you to let go of his clothing, your grabbing arm straightens. It is locked out against the joint and, as the circling move continues, the arm of the attacker is broken.

Different Types of Block

For the sake of effective learning, blocks in Ju-jitsu have been divided into the following areas:

- rising blocks;
- inside blocks;
- outside blocks;
- cover blocks;
- parries;
- lower area blocks; and
- cross (or 'x') blocks.

A rising block means that the blocking arm or hand is moving from the lower to the upper area in its execution. An inside block means that the blocking arm is moving from the inside of the body towards the outside. In an outside block, the blocking arm moves from the outside towards the inside. Some schools teach these the other way round.

In a cover block, you cover the opponent's fist or hand, whichever is more appropriate. The block is done with a downward movement. For example, when a punch is thrown towards your face, you step back and at the same time bring your hand in a cup shape over the top of the fist of the attacker. It is usually a prelude to taking hold of your attacker and is used very effectively in turning a punch against you into a wrist lock in your favour.

All blocking actions should be performed using the correct body position and stance, so that they can be executed to their maximum potential. Twisting strongly on the hips while performing a cross (or 'x') block makes the block much more efficient in terms of speed and power. The 'x' block is so called because it uses both arms, which form an 'x'. It is designed to trap and soften the oncoming blow, usually a downward strike to the head or a kick to the groin. As the attacker's arm or leg reaches the centre of the 'x', you can turn it into a capturing technique by twisting your body and arms.

Parries are deflections. A ball struck at an angle against a wall, for example, will bounce off to the side. The same principle is evident when a punch is coming towards you and you step to the side with a raised arm, allowing the punch to become a glancing blow off your arm. The punch misses you and has a minimal effect on your arm.

In all these techniques, the Ju-jitsu practitioner needs to be as relaxed and pliable as possible, ensuring swiftness of movement.

Examples of Blocks

The attacker (uke) is punching at the face of the defender (tori). An upper rising block is performed in an upper-cut movement and then finished with the blocking arm held at an angle in order to redirect the incoming blow. The blocking arm is twisted on its way up to meet the oncoming attack. At the point of contact with uke's arm, the back of tori's arm is facing towards him and about

Upper rising block.

15–25cm away from his head and face. The defender then counter-punches with a strike to his attacker's solar plexus.

Another attack to the face is blocked by a cross block, using the side edge of the forearm to block and at the same time protecting the face from another incoming punch. The entire forearm is utilized and brought across the upper body in a sweeping action. The fingers are clenched and facing the defender. This block is very powerful and the advanced practitioner can use it as a simultaneous attack to certain vital acupuncture points. Knowledge of these points is only for the most dedicated and true practitioner.

The downward forearm block is carried out against a front kick to the solar plexus or middle area. Again, this uses the outside of the forearm. The arm is brought from the right shoulder in a downward sweeping movement to block and strike the attacker's leg.

Cross block.

Downward forearm block.

'x' block.

An 'x' block (opposite) can be used against a kick and also a punch. A block such as this allows the defender to use both hands against a stronger opponent. As you advance in your skills you can use twisting and capturing techniques with this block.

An 's' block (below) is performed in order to pull the opponent off balance in preparation for a throw. Its action is to hook over and pull downward the punching arm; at the same time, the defender begins to move out of the way. The blocking arm is curved and should resemble the shape of a letter 's'.

The cover block (below) is a more advanced type, performed while leaning back from the strike. The striking arm is then covered and possibly captured.

The double forearm block (see page 54) is particularly useful against a kick. Both forms are used as a shield to protect against a powerful kick.

Strikes

In ancient times, the sword was always the most revered weapon but the development of Ju-jitsu enabled the Samurai to deal with offenders in less deadly fashion. Kicking techniques were developed and combined with various influences from other martial arts. The combination of striking techniques together with Ju-jitsu throws resulted in a devastating self-defence system. Ju-jitsu involves continuous movement, and the defender is able to adapt quickly from one

'S' block.

Cover block.

Double arm forearm block.

course of action, perhaps a block, to another, such as a lock, a strangle or a throw.

These techniques were (and still are) tempered by a spiritual understanding of the martial arts. Training in Ju-jitsu should enable the exponent to become an educator who provides the right environment for each individual's personal progress. He should encourage other students to develop a sense of worth, should be an inspiration to them and should care for every one of them. Sparring should always be introduced slowly and carefully supervised.

The code of Bushido is as relevant today as it was hundreds of years ago, including the virtues by which the Samurai lived, and died:

- gi, meaning the right decision or rectitude;

- yu, meaning valour;
- jin, benevolence;
- rei, the proper behaviour, courtesy, respect;
- makato, complete honesty;
- meiyo, honour and glory; and
- chugi, devotion and loyalty.

Some of the strikes and punches used in Ju-jitsu are more akin to those used by the boxer rather than by the Karate exponent, although straight-line punches are still used to great effect. Ju-jitsu practitioners must be able to strike from any angle and to a vulnerable area. You may have to strike while being held in chancery or when being pinned to the ground and straight-line punching is of no use in these circumstances. Confrontations usually start from less than 2m apart, and the ability to use hooks and close-quarter punching and striking is essential.

Basic Punching
Making a fist is one of the most basic forms of self-defence and a person who is angry or upset will often clench his fist without realizing it. Knowing how to punch and with which part of your hand is very important for two reasons: to avoid injury to your own hand, and to strike the target in the most effective way. As you clench your fist, make sure that the fingers are flat and not curled up inside the fist. This will protect the fingers from injury and will bring the two fore knuckles, with which you first learn to strike, into a more prominent position. Make sure that the thumb remains on the outside. Do not grip it!

The Ju-jitsu exponent should become well versed in the vulnerable striking areas of the human body (see diagrams opposite). The training in the striking of these areas is called atemi waza. Knowledge about atemi striking areas should be taught personally,

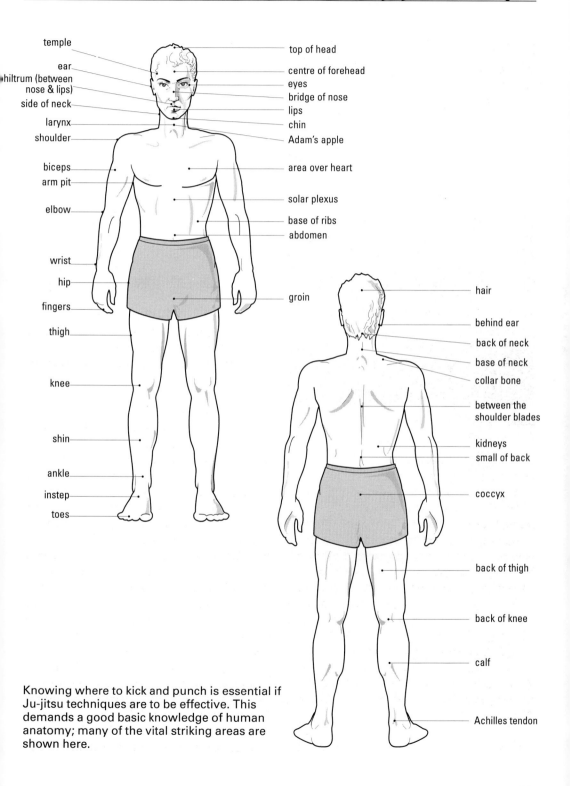

temple
ear
philtrum (between nose & lips)
side of neck
larynx
shoulder
biceps
arm pit
elbow
wrist
hip
fingers
thigh
knee
shin
ankle
instep
toes

top of head
centre of forehead
eyes
bridge of nose
lips
chin
Adam's apple
area over heart
solar plexus
base of ribs
abdomen
groin

hair
behind ear
back of neck
base of neck
collar bone
between the shoulder blades
kidneys
small of back
coccyx
back of thigh
back of knee
calf
Achilles tendon

Knowing where to kick and punch is essential if Ju-jitsu techniques are to be effective. This demands a good basic knowledge of human anatomy; many of the vital striking areas are shown here.

not from books or charts, and should be passed on only when the student has reached a certain level. In the early years, it is sufficient to show well-known striking points such as the groin or solar plexus.

Different Types of Strike

There are many varied strikes within Ju-jitsu, using different areas of the hand and attacking different areas of the opponent's body.

The knife hand strike, here given to the side of neck below, resembles the famous 'karate chop'. The strike was developed to enable the attacker to strike with maximum effect certain areas of the body that would be difficult to punch. A strike to the side of the neck can be very painful, but the actual target is the carotid artery, which, when struck,

could cause unconsciousness. Other areas where this striking technique could be used include the back of the neck, the groin, the collarbones, the temples and underneath the nose.

The one-side knuckle strike is here given to the cheekbone; the side-edge knuckle strike to the side of the jaw (opposite). Note the different way of holding the hand while striking in this way. Specifically targeting the joint of the jaw or mandible could case dislocation or even a break. The assailant's head has been forced sideways and this would also place a tremendous strain on the neck structures.

The palm-heel strike is a hand technique that is used a great deal in Ju-jitsu. Using the fleshy part of the heel of the hand protects the hand from injury. The strike given here

Knife hand strike (shuto).

One knuckle strike.

One knuckle strike.

Palm heel strike
(teisho).

is to the jaw (see p.57), made in an upward sweeping movement. This sort of strike could cause unconsciousness. The neck is angled in such a way that a whiplash-type dynamic injury could occur, along with damage to the cervical structure.

Elbow strikes may be made to the medul-la (base of skull) or to the neck (both below). As Ju-jitsu involves defence at very close quarters, the elbow is a useful tool that is commonly employed. In order to strike at the vital area of the neck, the initial attack usually has to be blocked, enabling the defender to get in close enough to use the

(Left) Elbow strike (empi)

(Below) Strike to meoula.

Knife hand strike.

Punch to throat.

elbow. The movement is similar to that of a punch, using only the elbow joint and the upper arm, in an upper-cut way, sweeping, downward or swinging backwards. The experienced practitioner will gain even greater advantage from such a strike by stepping away after the elbow strike, immediately straightening the arm, and then striking with a knife hand blow.

In the case of a knife hand strike to the opposite side of the neck, the defence could be continued by punching to the front of the attacker's throat with the right hand (both above). Such counter-strikes would be done in a rapid succession of moves, culminating in the opponent being struck three times.

When delivering a hammer fist strike,

here given to the bridge of nose, the hand is clenched tight and used in a downward hammering action. The hammer fist can be used to strike many large areas such as the temple, base of skull, kidney and spine.

Finger strikes to the eyes are a very effective defence. The idea is to blind your opponent temporarily, making it difficult for

Hammer fist strike (kentsui).

Finger strikes.

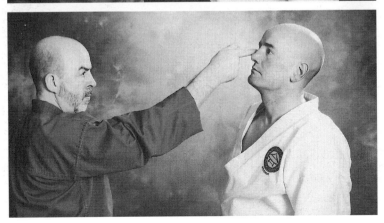

Finger strikes.

him to carry on with his attacks. This type of strike, like most of the others in this book, is illegal in competition (see Rules 16, 17 and 18, Forbidden Acts, pp. 113–14).

The back heel of hand strike, here given to the jaw , is a very strange-looking strike, using what is sometimes referred to as a 'chicken head wrist'. This strike is used from close quarters, striking upwards under your opponent's jaw.

In some martial arts, the half-clenched fist strike, here given to the throat (below), is called the 'tiger's paw', since it resembles a paw with claws retracted. It is a very useful strike as it enables you to attack small vulnerable areas such as the front of the throat. A large clenched fist would have difficulty in effectively striking such an area. The intercostals can also be struck very effectively with this particular 'punch'.

Back heel of hand strike.

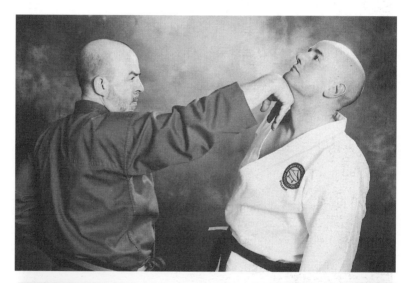

Half-clenched fist strike.

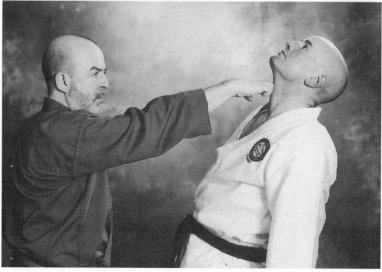

The inside knife hand strike, here delivered to the neck, uses the inside edge of the hand. It can be used in exactly the same way as the knife hand strike that uses the outside edge of the hand, to target vulnerable areas, but it can also be made with an upward motion if the hand is in a reversed or palm-upwards position.

The back fist strike, here delivered to the temple, is a big favourite among most martial artists, as it can be delivered with tremendous speed and accuracy. The emphasis is on the two knuckles of the first and middle fingers. As the arm bends back towards you, the wrist is whipped and locked out, and slightly bent, so that the

Inside knife hand.

Back fist strike (uraken).

two knuckles make contact with the target first.

Kicking

In the movies, martial artists often show off their kicking skills by standing on one leg, and kicking an assailant twenty times in the side of the head. In reality, this sort of attack is not practicable. Kicking skills are great for competition, when two exponents are standing off against each other about 2m apart, facing each other and sparring. This is not what confrontation is really like and these types of skill can become quite limited, although, if they are perfected, they can provide you with a formidable defensive weapon. The skilled exponent can decide to break or just push an attacker with a kick.

The technicalities of correct kicking need to be studied and practised. It is very different from kicking a football or Rugby ball, and is perhaps best described as a punch with the leg. The same mechanistic approach is used. To punch, you bend your arm at the elbow and then straighten it out. For most kicks, you bend the leg at the knee and snap it out to deliver the strike. Most people can kick to waist level and below and that is all that is required when targeting areas such as the stomach, groin or shin of the attacker.

The front snap kick to the solar plexus is performed with the toes bent back using the balls of the feet as the striking area, this is a very powerful kick. It is reminiscent of a punch in its action of the fast striking of the target and recoiling the leg back out of harm's way.

Front snap kick.

Side snap kick (yoko geri).

The side snap kick (yoko geri), here delivered to the knee in a typical use of this kick (see p.63), uses the outside edge of the foot. The foot is brought up to approximately the level of the knee. Maintaining your balance, try to turn the bottom of your kicking foot in towards your own standing leg, then snap the leg out against your target. With practice this kick can be delivered to the front as well as to the side. This kick can also be used in a thrusting manner, creating more of a push. For example, you can thrust sideways into your opponent's solar plexus using your body weight and momentum. This would wind the opponent and at the same time push him out of your way. Your kicking foot would land or be placed down in the same place where your opponent was standing. The snapping method would result in the kick being snapped out into your opponent's stomach and returning back to its starting position.

The back kick (Ushiro Geri) is shown here in its transitional stage, when the leg is still bent as it begins to thrust into the opponent's solar plexus. On impact, the leg straightens, causing the opponent to be knocked backwards or to the ground. This is a very good effective kick when being attacked from behind. If delivered correctly, it would incapacitate most attackers as it utilizes one of the most powerful leg muscles (the quadriceps).

The roundhouse kick (Mawashi Geri) (opposite) uses either the balls of the feet or instep to strike the opponent's upper regions. Good stretching and flexibility are the key to perfecting this kick.

Back kick

Roundhouse kick.

The blocks and kicks described above are useful against very basic attacks, and may be performed by most people of all ages. High kicks tend to be used only in an open sparring forum between students in the dojo, or in other martial art competitions, and they do not represent a major part of Ju-jitsu's defensive system.

7 Advancement of Ju-Jitsu Techniques

Locking

The locking of an opponent's joints is a very effective and painful way of immobilizing him from doing further harm. In Ju-jitsu it is an integral part of the skills needed, most throws either beginning with a lock or ending with a lock, or both. Being able to block an opponent's punch and then lock the punching arm is a powerful combat skill. The lock is is usually against the natural movement of the joint. In Ju-jitsu it is quite usual to learn locking skills against wrists, fingers, arms, elbows, shoulders, legs and knees, and even spinal locks are taught in some syllabuses.

Locking a joint really equates to a hold – the opponent is held in a position that restrains him from attempting to make a further attack.

Wrist Locks

In a wrist lock, the wrist of the opponent is held in a position in which it will not move any further through its natural range. The arm may be held at the same time, in a blocked or straight-arm position, and then pressure is applied direct through the wrist. In using a wrist lock in a self-defence situation, the aim is to gain control of the aggressor through pain compliance. It allows control without inflicting pain, yet gives the option of applying the lock and creating pain if necessary.

Wrist lock and kick to vital area.

A wrist lock can be used while kicking to a vital area (see opposite), with the kicking being a fundamental part of the technique. It allows the practitioner to weaken the attacker, making the wrist lock easier to apply and much more effective. As they say, 'pain confuses the brain'. After the initial shock of being hurt, the attacker now has two points of pain, and the extra pain is being administered on a control and restraint basis. The whole scenario is mentally and physically debilitating and humiliating to the attacker, who is likely to submit and stop struggling.

A number of wrist locks are possible, including the reverse wrist lock, which shows that the joint of the wrist can be locked against itself in various ways. When applied correctly, this lock forces the opponent to the ground as he is withdrawing from the pain being administered. His only avenue of movement is in the opposite direction from the application of the lock. Kicking to a vital area is again an integral part of the technique.

In this defence against a double wrist grab (see p.68), the attacker has grabbed both

Reverse wrist lock.

Defence against a double wrist grab.

Turns left palm upwards and steps to the left.

Twists the attacker's wrist, forcing him to the ground.

wrists. The defender quickly turns his left hand palm upwards and steps to the side, so that if the attacker decides to kick out at the last second, the defender is less likely to be injured. The movement enables him to grab the attacker's right wrist. The powerful twisting motion which then follows results in the attacker releasing his grip and allows the defender to complete the technique by forcing him to the ground.

Combining a bent elbow and wrist lock involves the application of pressure directly through the wrist and forearm. The opponent's elbow is placed against your sternum and held in that position (by the left arm in this case). The wrist is bent downwards. This move should be done with extreme caution. Pressure should be applied very gently and your opponent or training partner should tap your arm or the floor to let you

Bent elbow and wrist lock.

Side angle wrist lock.

know when any more pressure would be unacceptable.

The side angle wrist lock (see p.69) uses the wrist against the joint in an upward movement. When the opponent attempts to take hold of your jacket, you quickly grab his wrist and hand in a 'praying' grip. The little finger on his hand is uppermost and your intention is to force the wrist to bend towards his little finger. This action and the pain that it creates causes the attacker to bend his knees in a crouching manner, in order to avoid further pain, and a kick to his solar plexus can then be performed.

The 'figure 4 thrust lock' is exactly the same as the bent elbow and wrist lock, except that it is applied when the opponent has been thrown to the ground. His head is pinned with your left knee and his pelvic girdle with your right knee while the lock is being applied. More pressure can be applied to the opponent's mastoid process with your right knee, making him more compliant.

Arm Locks

(Some of these locks are applied while immobilizing the opponent's head with the knee.)

To perform the shoulder arm and wrist lock, keeping hold of the opponent's wrist with your right hand, twist his arm so that his palm is facing upwards. His arm is now

Figure 4 thrust lock.

Shoulder arm and wrist lock.

held in a position against the elbow joint. Then wrap your left arm over his arm, grip your own wrist, and apply a downward levering pressure to your opponent's wrist and elbow joint.

In the shoulder arm lock the pressure is in a downward motion. Push the wrist against the joint while at the same time immobilizing the elbow and shoulder joints with your left arm and body. Note the strong stance taken up by the person applying the lock in order to avoid the opponent pulling away or placing him off balance during the procedure.

In the second shoulder arm lock, the opponent has tried to grab the other's left arm at the shoulder. He has swung his left arm in a circular movement, at the same time placing his right hand on his attacker's shoulder. The left arm continues its movement and catches hold of his own arm and wrist. The pressure is then applied at the attacker's elbow joint and shoulder.

(Left) Shoulder arm lock.

Shoulder arm lock.

Figure 4 back hammer lock.

The figure 4 back hammer lock is so called because the arms resemble a number '4'. The principle is the same as in all the other similar types of lock, with pressure being applied through the wrist and shoulder joints. This lock makes the attacker bend forward as the arm is forced further up the back, and he could then be taken right down to the ground.

In principle, the bent arm and shoulder lock is a reverse figure 4 lock, although the pressure is applied differently. The opponent's hand and forearm are being held under the other's arm. His right arm is pushing the attacker's elbow while he takes hold of his own wrist with his left hand. The more he pushes, the more he creates pain at the attacker's shoulder joint. At the same time,

(Right) Bent arm and shoulder lock.

he is pinning the head and body in order to control the attacker.

In the particular shoulder arm lock shown below the attacker is being pinned to the ground by his head and hip. The lock is applied against the elbow joint, and the shoulder is secured and locked to make sure that there is no movement of the joint.

A straight-arm bar (see right) is performed by pushing the opponent's elbow joint against your own leg. The attacker is then thrown on to his side or back. The defender is already in a strong stance, with the front knee bent. It is important to keep control of the attacker's arm when he has been thrown to the ground. The lock is applied to the opponent's elbow joint using the bent knee as a pivotal point.

Straight-arm bar.

Shoulder arm lock.

Shoulder, elbow and wrist lock arm trap.

A variation of the shoulder, elbow and wrist lock arm trap.

The shoulder, elbow and wrist lock (see p.73) is sometimes referred to as a 'cricket bat lock', since it resembles the grip used on a cricket bat when blocking the ball. Pressure is applied down through the wrist, against the elbow joint, with the knee against the shoulder. The opponent is forced over on his side and his other arm is trapped underneath his own body. At this stage the defender could even step on the attacker's outstretched arm in order to immobilize him completely.

The arm trap (opposite) is a variation of the shoulder, elbow and wrist lock.

There are many times in competition when locks have to be applied while you are on the ground, and the straight-arm lock, performed here against the elbow joint, is one of the most useful. It can be applied straight from throwing your opponent. Stepping over his body, sit down, lie back, and apply the lock. Your left leg stops the opponent from coming up off the ground and taking the pressure off.

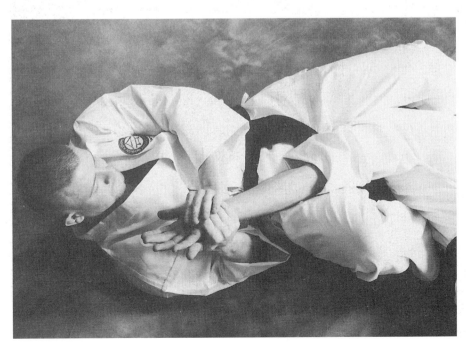

Straight-arm lock.

The opponent is restrained by a double arm lock and head hold), with both arms locked. He is controlled by holding him against his jaw and the application of pressure towards the back of his head, against the arm of the defender.

This double arm lock and head hold is the same as the first, but this time the leg is used.

The double arm lever against both shoulder joints (see p.76) is a very useful technique when your opponent has been thrown, or has landed face down. By quickly catching hold of his wrists you can lever the shoulder joints up. It will be virtually impossible for him to move if this lock is applied correctly. At this point you could even slide down the arms and sit astride your opponent and apply.

The double arm lever immobilizes the opponent's body.

In performing this single shoulder arm and wrist lock, the foot is pushed under the attacker's neck and the lock is applied by pushing down in a straight line through the wrist. The wrist is then twisted towards his head, creating a torque on the whole arm. The foot under the opponent's jaw is acting as a sort of lock, making sure that he cannot move his head and body without more pain.

In this single shoulder arm and wrist lock, if you simply maintain hold of the opponent's arm you can move quickly in to another lock, while restraining the attacker with your foot across the side of his neck, and sitting back on him.

To defend against your opponent grabbing both your wrists from behind, kick to his groin, turn swiftly and, keeping hold of his wrist, grab his elbow with your free right hand. The bent arm and wrist lock (see

Double arm lock and head hold.

Double arm lock and head hold.

Double arm lever.

Double arm lever.

Single shoulder arm and wrist lock.

Single shoulder arm and wrist lock.

Defence against a rear double wrist grab with a back heel to the groin.

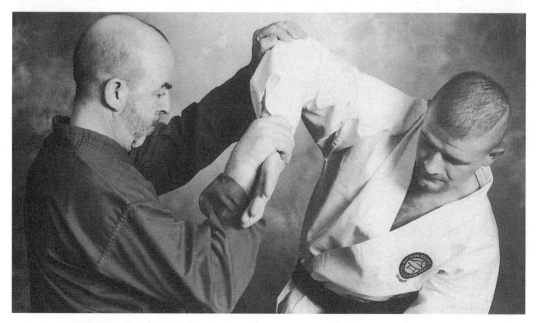

Bent arm and wrist lock.

Shoulder arm bar and lever lock.

p.77) is the transition stage of this technique. Keep moving in a circular fashion, then move into and apply the shoulder arm bar and lever lock.

After the shoulder arm and wrist lock has been applied, when the opponent starts to struggle, turning your body will cause his arm to bend, enabling you to apply the elbow and wrist lock (see opposite). The elbow is pressed hard against the sternum while you hold your own wrist. You can then apply considerable pressure straight through the wrist joint.

Strangles and Chokes

A strangle cuts off the blood supply to the brain whereas a choke cuts off the air supply to the lungs. A strangle is sometimes much more effective than a choke, since the opponent may have lungs full of air and there may be some delay before it is used up. If the blood supply is slowed or stopped, the brain automatically shuts down in order to protect itself and there is a shortage of oxygen carried by the blood.

Shoulder arm and wrist lock.

Elbow and
wrist lock.

Side strangle and shoulder arm lock.

In performing the side strangle and shoulder arm lock, use the jacket across the side of the neck and at the same time trap the opponent's right arm under your arm. Place your left leg at the back of his neck, locking his left arm. He is now immobilized and, as you apply pressure to the side of his head, the collar of the jacket is brought against his carotid artery, restricting the blood flow to the brain.

For the choke and shoulder lock (see p.80), bring your opponent's right arm across your chest while you are kneeling down. Place your right leg over his left arm and trap it. Bring your right arm across his windpipe and take hold of your own opposite wrist.

In the reverse neck lock and strangulation (see p.80), your opponent is taken from behind and pressure is applied across the carotid artery while the neck is forced backwards.

The bar choke (see p.80) involves the right hand forming a bar across the windpipe of the opponent. Grip as high up on the opponent's collar as you can, push your

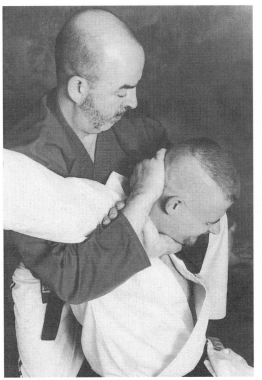

Choke and shoulder lock.

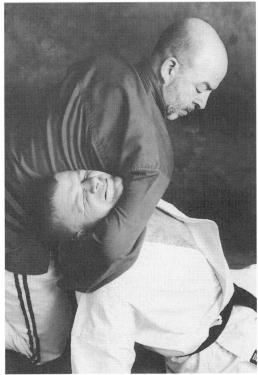

Reverse neck lock and strangulation.

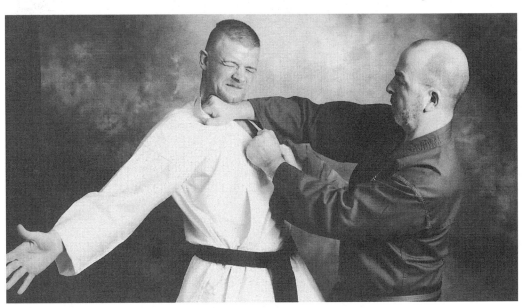

Bar choke.

forearm across his throat, and pull him towards you by gripping his jacket with your other arm.

The straight-arm lock and strangulation is a technique that is performed when the attacker has grabbed your arm. Swing over his left arm and trap it between your own arm and body. At the same time quickly grip your opponent's epiglottis. To create a more stable lock make sure that your left arm is under the elbow joint of his arm and that you are gripping your own arm. Pressure is applied up through the elbow joint and to the throat.

In this back hammer and choke, the opponent's arm has been forced up his back and is held between the other's left forearm and bicep. The right arm is then brought across the opponent's throat and the fingers are hooked together; the 'finger grip' makes for a better hold.

Straight-arm lock and strangulation.

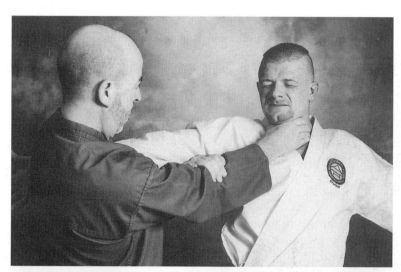

Back hammer and choke.

8 Ground-Fighting Techniques

The term 'ground fighting' has been very much in vogue in the last few years, but there is nothing new in the techniques. Many martial arts, from Judo or Ninjitsu to the Filipino arts, have some form of 'ground combat' within their system, and it is only the rules for each specific competition that vary.

There has been a significant increase in ground-fighting schools and competitions, and many top-ranking true martial artists have continued to research the history, foundations and effectiveness of ground fighting. Practitioners have been putting more and more emphasis on ground fighting since 80 per cent of real-life confrontations inevitably end up on the floor and, unless the practitioner is prepared for this, he will certainly have problems. The sight of two Ju-jitsu combatants fighting on the ground today is little different from scenes that would have been witnessed in battle hundreds of years ago.

The Ju-jitsu practitioner is a blended warrior of fighting systems. He is not limited by having to use one specific counter to one technique, but will be able to flow from one technique to another, on 'automatic pilot'. When one technique begins to fail, he is already moving inspirationally into another.

The Ju-jitsu student should be like a sponge, absorbing all aspects of ground fighting inside his own system. As he develops, he should study other systems. He should learn to be selective, yet should keep an open mind and true heart. The Ju-jitsu practitioner is not trying to learn many different martial arts, but there are strong similarities between the systems. (An arm lock is an arm lock, whichever system it belongs to.) The Ju-jitsu practitioner should aim to make himself aware of the variations between the systems, and of the differing applications. For every lock there is a counter and it is the exploration of the counters of various locks in various systems that builds the repertoire of the experienced practitioner. In order to become a master in Ju-jitsu, it is necessary to examine, explore and experiment with other systems and styles.

The major difference between fighting standing up and grappling on the ground is the fact that you can use your legs as effectively as your arms – you are still able to kick and punch while on the ground in a real fight situation. Differences in height are not such a problem when fighting on the ground, although weight can make a difference between two skilled practitioners.

Using Technique

The Ju-jitsu student should practise these skills regularly, giving as much time to them as to the rest of his required training. There are certain challenges in fighting on the ground in an outside confrontation. There are no soft mats on the floor. The clothing is likely to be poorly suited to grappling. There is no teacher to supervise or say stop. If you have been pushed or even thrown to the ground you may already be injured, or lying in an unusual body position. Your attacker may be intent on doing you real harm. The environment may be wet, dirty, or dangerous, with glass on the floor or furniture in the way.

For all these reasons, it is essential for the Ju-jitsuka to learn his skills well. In unusual situations and in a difficult environment the practitioner must be able to rely on his good technique and understand the principles that allow him to use his energies wisely. The use of the body is very important in Ju-jitsu ground-fighting skills. Attributes that come into play include speed, strength, positioning; however, the longer a fight goes on, strength and speed begin to decline, and only technique is left. If the technique has not been practised diligently, winning becomes less of an option. Coordination and timing are vital, otherwise the fighting simply involves two people rolling around on the floor, trying to keep from being hurt. Ju-jitsu teaches throwing, as well as rolling or breakfalling to avoid injury. When someone is thrown to the ground his first instinct is to try to get up. If you know the techniques, you can take the person with you to the ground as you are being thrown, and can turn misfortune into advantage.

Real-Life Applications

Being knocked to the ground makes an individual very vulnerable to attack, but a good Ju-jitsu exponent, who is accomplished in some basic grappling techniques, should be able to turn this to his advantage.

In Ju-jitsu we develop skills, attributes and abilities to the point where, if misused, they can be very dangerous. We must understand that they are developed as a deterrent to victimization or from physical attack as in self-defence. Development of our internal abilities is also essential so that we are perceived as strong and self-confident.

Therefore we stand a much greater chance of not being preyed upon by those who prey upon the weak.

In the USA some police forces are now teaching specific forms of ground fighting as a defensive tactic. Until the early 1980s such tactics were virtually unheard of. As police trainers began to recognize the need for such strategies they turned to martial arts instructors. Many martial arts disciplines already had ground-fighting systems in place, and these were taught to police trainers.

Because most martial arts at that time were kick-oriented, it was recommended that students fight while lying on one side, using one leg and two arms as a base, and using the free leg to attack. Mobility was achieved by rocking from side to side, shuffling back or forward on one hip, or crab walking using all four limbs. The general philosophy of these systems was to attack until you could get up, and to get up as soon as possible. (The commonly held view was that if the officer was not able to get up on his feet within 10 to 30 seconds, he would lose the fight.)

In the specific ground-fighting systems that have been designed for police officers and law enforcement agencies, the officer learns to fight on his back, in an almost foetal position. Movement is circular rather than linear. This technique was put to good use by an American police officer in foot pursuit of an armed suspect. The suspect was chased on to a railway platform, where he stopped and turned towards the officer. The officer slid on his back and, using both feet, pinned the suspect to the wall. Each time the suspect attempted to reach down to his ankle holster for his firearm, the officer peppered him with kicks, making him straighten up again. Because he was on his back, the officer was able to reach for both his radio and his firearm, and called for back-up.

There has been much debate among trainers of defensive tactics over which system (back or side) is better for police officers. Ground fighting on one side looks more impressive and aggressive, but is it as effective? Some claim that kicking has more impact when lying on the side, but studies show otherwise. The 'back position' offers more offence and defence in more directions than the 'side position'. The side position leaves the officer's spine and head more vulnerable while the back position allows the ground to protect the spine and the hands and arms to protect the head. This is especially important in multiple assailant confrontation, when even a moderate kick to the spinal area (from the base of the skull to the coccyx) can render the arms or legs useless. Such damage could cause long-term or permanent disability.

The side position depends heavily on linear movement and rocking for mobility, and this can cause the officer's firearm to be scraped or bumped along the ground, or dislodge his baton. It can also leave the arms very susceptible to attack and serious injury. The position also leaves the baton or firearm pinned to the ground and inaccessible. The circular motion of some systems uses less energy and can be accomplished easily with the use of only one limb, or even none. Leaving both arms free, it also allows for effective use of the baton or firearm. The back position keeps the baton and the firearm low, close to the ground, allowing the officer to use either of them effectively in all directions, or to fire without losing accuracy.

Recovery (getting up) from the side position is also more difficult, requiring the officer to place one or both hands on the ground and retreat. This could prove dangerous if there are other assailants at the scene. The back position allows the officer to get up without placing either hand on the ground,

and to use his baton or firearm during the process.

The biggest difference in the two systems is the general strategy. The side-position system was developed with a view to the fact that the martial artist must get up as soon as possible and is unlikely to be dealing with multiple assailants. The police officer may be on the ground due to a broken or injured leg (or legs) and is likely to be dealing with more than one assailant.

A good ground-fighting system also teaches the officer that, when he hits the ground, the fight is not necessarily over; in fact, it is just beginning. Traditionally, officers have been taught that falling to the ground in a confrontation is dangerous and undesirable. However, with the right mindset and training, falling may be a good tactical move. Officers need to understand that falling is not losing. In order to develop the skills for getting to the ground safely, as part of a survival strategy, an officer needs to engage in realistic training. A suitable law enforcement ground-fighting programme should address blocking, weapon retention, access of equipment, escapes from holds, multiple assailants and ground mobility. Falling safely can prevent injuries from accidents, and is the doorway to an effective style of combat.

At first, falling and ground fighting can feel awkward and uncomfortable, but once you become familiar with your new environment, you will find a whole new world of possibilities. If the assailant is less comfortable in that environment, you have a tremendous advantage. Many officers, after a little training and a change of mind-set, actually prefer to fight from the ground in some situations.

Remember, getting up from the ground is not the ultimate goal in a ground-fighting situation. You should get up only when it is safe to get up. The goal remains the same as in any other violent confrontation – to win the fight.

Randori

The average Ju-jitsu student should train at least twice a week and part of that training should involve an introduction to randori.

Randori means 'free practice' and allows the student to experience being held down or strangled, or being placed under various locks, all in a safe environment. Each individual is also trying to do the same to his training partner. Randori is usually introduced when students have a certain level of understanding of some of the basic principles of Ju-jitsu. These pretend fight situations may be daunting at first but with extreme caution and mutual respect they can be great fun. There is a good sense of achievement when your partner is unable to move, or do anything, because you have successfully immobilized him.

Various Techniques

A head and arm immobilization is performed here. The attacker (right) is being stopped from grabbing with his right hand, while the defender (left) is pulling down on

(Above and below) Head and arm immobilization.

Neck brace and strangle.

Push-over.

Strangle and neck brace.

Straight-arm lever.

Neck strike and push-over.

Ground strangulation.

the arm that has already succeeded in grabbing his jacket. The defender has successfully turned the attacker on to his back and now applies an immobilizing head and arm hold.

The attacker (left) pushes his opponent on to his back (opposite), and quickly applies a neck brace and strangle.

For the straight-arm lever), the attacker (right) pushes the defender on to his back.

The defender quickly spins and places his left leg across the attacker's neck pushing him over in a neck strike and push-over (see p.87). This culminates in the defender being able to execute a straight-arm lever on his attacker.

The attacker on the left has his head pushed down as he rushes in. This is quickly turned into a ground strangulation technique (below).

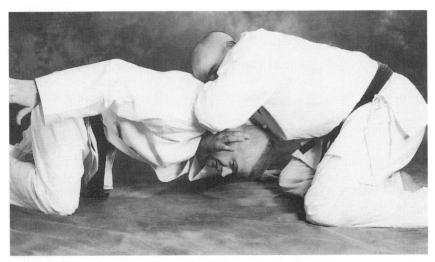

Intermediate stage: the attacker has his head pushed down.

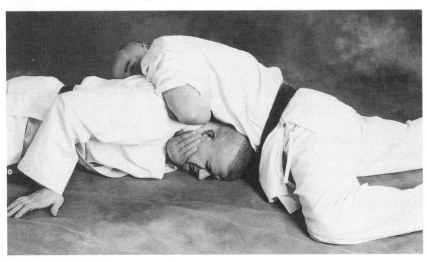

Ground strangulation.

9 Defensive Principles of Ju-Jitsu

Hapkido, which means 'coordinated power', is a Korean martial art that is characterized by kicking without retraction, and a total penetration of the opponent's defences. It uses a non-violent code of counter-defence, which leads to fluid circular motion and constant mobility. Some of its foundations and traditional moves are inextricably linked with the art of Ju-jitsu.

Martial artists are trained continually to develop and refine their self-defence skills, and the training often involves drills. The defensive tactics generally taught by many martial art systems teach you how to defend yourself with forceful techniques once an opponent has already grabbed hold of you, or has unleashed an attack such as a kick or a punch. Defending yourself at this stage of an attack is problematic, because your opponent either already has a hold of you, or has already punched or kicked you. Ju-jitsu teaches you how to move, block, strike, throw and restrain.

Ju-jitsu is based on the assumption that, in many cases, your opponent will at some stage take hold of you. In addition to this if your attacker has already begun to punch at you, that punch is in motion – it has power, and speed – and in many martial arts you can only hope to defend against it with a traditional block. The traditional Korean martial art system of Hapkido teaches its practitioners to defend themselves before their attacker has the opportunity to solidify his attack.

Theory of Circular Self-Defence

In order to achieve self-defence in the early stages of an attack, traditional Hapkido uses its Theory of Circular Self-Defence. This is closely related to the teaching of Ju-jitsu and prefers avoidance, either by circular or other movements, to hard blocking.

Circular self-defence, epitomized in other martial arts such as Aikido, does not involve moving your body in elaborate and exaggerated circular movements. It is twofold. First, it teaches that the most important element in any confrontation is to define the range from which your opponent is attacking. This takes a lot of practice and understanding. In other words, a risk assessment of the situation is quickly made. The knowledge is then used to select the most appropriate and effective self-defence measure, which is put into place before the opponent can launch a successful attack.

Once the range is defined, the second level of the theory can be addressed, that of moving a in fluid circular motion.

In order to define the range of your opponent's attack, you use the Three Concentric Circle Principle.

The principle involves a visualization of three circles of varying radii encompassing your body. The First, or Primary, Circle extends around you for approximately 1m, or the distance of your outstretched arms. If an opponent has initiated an attack within the primary circle, immediate and aggressive self-defence is necessary. This is the stage at which he has most likely thrown a punch or grabbed you, or both.

The Second Circle ranges from 1m to 2m around your body. At this level, your opponent needs to travel to you in order to launch an effective attack, and this requires a certain amount of momentum. This momentum can be used effectively against him, by deflecting his forward motion and using his expended energy to your own advantage. In Ju-jitsu a circular fluid parrying action is used to deflect the attack. This can either be turned into a throw or a counter-strike, or just a simple avoidance.

Certain circumstances dictate that you must travel to your opponent, for example, if you have your back to a wall. If you have to cross the second circle limit, you must do so in a balanced offensive posture. The second circle is relatively close, and many martial artists attempt to over-stretch close-in punching or kicking techniques to this 1–2m distance. This is a mistakes, as it will leave you off balance. If you do not make successful contact, your attacker can use your lack of balance to his own advantage and strike you with a powerful attack. Once you are sufficiently accomplished, you will be able to counter immediately with an appropriate powerful strike such as a straight punch followed by a joint lock and throw.

The Third, or Tertiary, Circle extends from 2m to 3m around your body. If your opponent travels this distance to attack you, his oncoming motion is very obvious and appropriate defensive action can easily be prepared for and instigated. If, on the other hand, you decide it is in your best interest to travel this distance and encounter your opponent where he is located, then you must do so in the most efficient manner possible. However, there is no reason to travel this sort of distance towards any opponent. If he

is armed with a weapon, he will not be able to hit you from that distance.

First defining the range of your opponent's attack allows you to enter into any confrontation prepared to defend yourself in the most appropriate manner. This is known as range-effective fighting. Once the range of your defensive posture is understood you can successfully employ the second area of circular self-defence, that of circular movement.

Avoidance Techniques (Furimi Waza)

Body movement is directly connected to the success of every technique in Ju-jitsu. Although footwork is limited to the movements of the legs and feet, dynamic body movement broadens considerably when it includes avoiding or shifting of position to avoid an attack and to set up for counter-attack. Developing advanced skill in avoidance techniques (Furimi Waza) is an essential part of traditional Ju-jitsu.

There are nine basic types of avoidance technique to master in traditional Ju-jitsu:

1. Avoiding by stepping (kaishin);
2. Avoiding by stepping to the side (yoko furimi);
3. Avoiding by stepping backwards (sorimi);
4. Avoiding by a pull-in (hikimi);
5. Avoiding by a circular movement (ryusui);
6. Avoiding by performing a jumping retreat (tobi sagari);
7. Avoiding by a sliding retreat (hiraki sagari);
8. Avoiding by a using a full-turn (zen tenkan);
9. Avoiding by using a half-turn (hon tenkan).

Kaishin

This is a movement technique in which the

Ju-jitsuka moves one foot in order to avoid the attacker's assault. The technique may be executed in two ways:

1. Moving one foot in a circular manner to the rear so as to turn the upper body to the side and avoid the initial attack;
2. Stepping forward diagonally to the side with one foot and turn the body towards the attacker.

Yoko Furimi

This technique moves only the upper body to the side without moving the feet. It is designed to avoid an attacker's punch, kick or strike towards the head. The hands must continue to provide centre-line coverage to allow for blocking and quick counterattack.

Sorimi

In this technique, the body weight is shifted to the rear leg and the upper body is leant backwards, without moving the feet, to avoid the attacker's punch, kick or strike to the upper body. The Ju-jitsuka's balance must be maintained to facilitate kick counterattacks.

Hikimi

In this technique, the body weight is shifted to the rear, but only the middle part of the body is retracted, in order to avoid the attacker's kick and/or punch to the stomach. The hands must continue to provide centre-line coverage to allow for blocking and quick counterattack.

Ryusui

The feet do not move, but the body drops and moves to the side in a circular manner to avoid the attacker's punch, kick or strike to the upper body. The arms are positioned to block any kicks by the attacker.

Tobi Sagari

In this movement techniqu, the Ju-jitsuka must exercise extreme alertness to the potential attack. At the moment when the attacker begins his forward motion assault, the Ju-jitsuka executes a jump to the rear to avoid the initial attack. Upon landing from the jump, the Ju-jitsuka must maintain balance in order to execute a counterattack.

Hiraki Sagari

This technique is similar to the jumping retreat, except that the feet slide along the ground. Timing, proper distance and the ability to execute a counterattack are equally important when using this technique.

Zen Tenkan

This movement technique is used when in close quarters with an attacker. As the attacker grasps or thrusts towards the upper body, the Ju-jitsuka quickly moves one foot in a circular manner (180 degrees), while pivoting on the other foot. This technique can be used as a set-up for a throw (nage waza) or to avoid a choke or grab by the attacker.

Hon Tenkan

This technique is used to protect the 'vital points' of the body. As the attacker punches kicks or grabs, one foot moves in a circular manner (90 degrees), while pivoting on the other foot. A blocking technique should be executed during the dodge. After executing the half-turn dodge, the Ju-jitsuka is in a good position to counterattack.

Immobilizing and Disengagement Techniques

The art of disengagement is a complex and skilled part of Ju-jitsu. It is a system of countermeasures against techniques such as hold or locks that are about to be applied or are being applied. The best way to learn these techniques is in a class situation.

Many attacks are from grabs, either of clothing or of body extremities such as hands, arms, neck and head, and grabs are usually followed up by punches. Awareness at all times is vital. In Ju-jitsu training it is common to develop exercises that speed up the reflexes and improve response times to many situations and attacks. Diligent training gives you the ability to respond correctly to being grabbed, and then kicked or punched, and the chance to turn a potentially hopeless situation into one of defence or escape. Will you want to immobilize such an opponent? In many cases, it would be preferable to get away, but if releasing your attacker would leave you vulnerable to fur-

ther attacks, it might be better to hang on in there.

Examples of Defence Techniques

An attack attempting strangulation from the front would be very distressing to the majority of people and panic would almost always set in. The individual here has been involved in repetitive training, so her response is one of instinctive movement rather than a slow deliberate thought process. She immediately steps back into a strong stance and at the same time strikes the attacker's jaw with the heel of her hand while pulling sharply down on his right elbow. (The strong stance is a very important aspect of the defence system. It keeps you balanced, which is important if the

Defence against strangulation from the front.

Transitional arm lock.

(Above and right) Defence against a rear neck grab.

attacker has got hold of you.) This causes a circular movement of the attacker's body, which pulls him off balance and on to the ground. Using a transitional arm lock (see opposite), the defender has successfully controlled the attacker's arm that she pulled down. She must now immediately immobilize him with either a lock or, in this case, a strike to a vulnerable area.

The rear neck grab is another common attack. As she is grabbed by the neck from behind, the defender strikes to the attacker's groin which causes pain and gives her the split seconds that she requires to disengage herself and turn the situation into a positive one. She has also taken hold of his wrist at the same time as striking. His grip is now much weaker and she is able to bend the arm away and lock it underneath her right arm. This elbow and shoulder lock causes severe pain through the elbow and shoulder joints of the attacker.

Elbow and shoulder lock.

Defence against a side strangulation.

Hip throw and figure 4 thrust lock.

In this side strangulation the attacker is concerned only with his attack and does not really contemplate much resistance. His stance is open and this gives the victim the opening that she has been trained to seek. She immediately strikes to the attacker's groin. This is extremely painful and would have the desired effect of loosening his grip. She is then able to disengage herself from the grip and to complete her move by turning into and performing a basic hip throw and figure 4 thrust lock.

The figure 4 thrust lock and neck restraint will immobilize an attacker. The lock is very powerful and controls the arm of the aggressor while pressure is applied against and through the wrist, using the chest as a fulcrum or stop.

Figure 4 thrust lock and neck restraint.

There are many ways of immobilizing an opponent. The majority involve either the locking of joints to create pain or actually rendering the attacker unconscious.

A Progression of Ju-Jitsu Techniques

Hip Throw

In the basic approach stance for a hip throw, the knees are slightly bent and the opponent is held very tight. This is a particularly good example of circular movement. A punch has been thrown in the area that you have to defend. A circular blocking action is performed in unison with your body turning in a full circle and bending. The effect is that the attacker's body weight is thrown forward, first by the momentum of his punch and then by this movement being continued by the circular capturing-type block. The action of bending cause the person to lose balance even more and disrupts his point of balance.

Inside Hock Throw

After successfully defending against a punch, the defender strikes to the attacker's throat and steps inside his legs. She hooks her leg around the back of his and straightens it at the same time as the strike, causing the attacker to fall backwards. The block used is an avoidance type, with the strike glancing off your arm. Shifting your body position makes the block even more effective, as the attacker falls on to your strike.

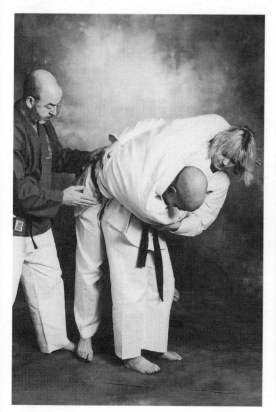

Hip throw.

Inside hock throw.

The weakening effect of the strike to the throat, coupled with the inability of the attacker to move in any direction other than backwards, makes this a very powerful and most effective Ju-jitsu technique.

Defence against a Front Kick

The attacker has swung a kick with all his force in a straight line, and the defender sweeps away the leg on which he is standing. The defender has first and foremost avoided the attack by positioning her body sideways in a semi-circular movement. She would initially have had both her arms up in a defensive posture. As she moves, she guards the side of her body that was nearer to the kick and swings her arm under the attacker's knee. She continues her circular movement

by grabbing and pushing and stepping through her opponent's point of balance. She is now in a position to take her attacker straight on to his back.

Dropping Version of a Body Drop Throw

The same position is taken up as in body drop, only this time your centre of gravity is now lower and you push up with one hand under the attacker's arm and pull down on his other arm, bringing him over your out stretched leg

A Back Hock Throw

After blocking the opponent's punch you step forward and kick backwards behind his leg, whilst pulling on his punching arm and

Defence against a front kick.

Dropping version of a body drop throw.

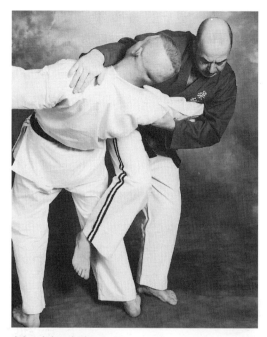

A back hock throw.

pushing on his other shoulder in a twisting movement.

A Leg Throw with an Applied Leg Lock.
Block the attack and quickly bend down grabbing the attacker's ankle and at the same time as you lift his leg you are pushing him with your forearm at the top of his leg, causing him to be taken off balance and fall on his back. You can then apply the leg lock as shown.

'Front Scoop'
The attacker (left, p.98) is stopped from grabbing by the defender using a wedge-type blocking action. The defender quickly grabs his jacket and scoops under the attacker's groin, lifting and dropping him on to the base of his neck.

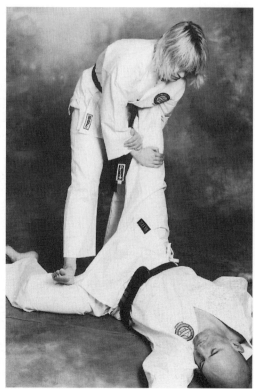

A leg throw with an applied leg lock.

Grab the leg and push down with your forearm.

Blocking the attempted grab.

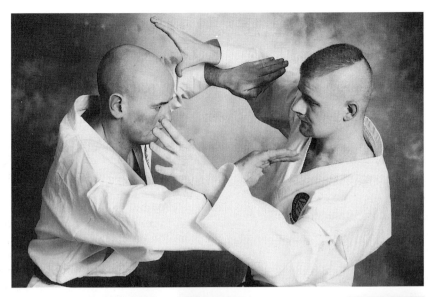

Hold lapel, push back and thrust arm under groin.

Scoop and drop attacker on base of neck.

10 Weapons in Ju-Jitsu

The Sword (Katana)

The Samurai sword, or katana, was a classic weapon that has never lost its notoriety. The sword was manufactured in such a way as to be as strong and as sharp as possible, yet easy to handle with just one hand. There were various sizes of sword and many fighting systems developed around the use of the weapon.

Kenjutsu is the art of using the techniques of the sword whilst Iajutsu is the art of drawing, cutting and sheathing the sword as quickly as possible, as in a duel.

History
The history of the Japanese sword dates back to the seventh and eighth centuries, with bevel-edged swords appearing at some time around the seventh century. The Japanese swordsmiths were among the finest in the world and their techniques for the forging of the sword were closely guarded secrets. The sword has always played a part in the spirituality of Japan and its people. It is also part of the imperial regalia, first worn and given to the Emperor Ameteratsu, who was known as the sun goddess and was the founder of the Imperial Line.

Originally, the sword was manufactured from up to 9,000 strata of steel, folded, mul-tiplied and cross-laminated. This created a blade with varying degrees of hardness. A higher or lower carbon content was hammered to create extraordinary toughness. Later, the sword was forged from a single block of steel, and the blades could be catalogued or made to individual specifications, with regard to the hardness of the steel. Using this technique, the swordsmith was able to produce an incredibly light, hard and extremely sharp blade. It was at about the same time, around 796–1187, that the sword was given the gentle curve shape for which it is famous.

A swordsmith usually lived a religious and dedicated life, and was often a member of a sect or school. Early examples could be traced back to a specific school and even to the master swordsmith himself. Many of the swords bore identification marks. The swordsmith would also engrave his signature into the tang of the sword, so that it was possible to trace where and when a sword was made, and by whom.

Periods of Sword-Making
The swords can be catalogued to several periods in Japan's history:

• Jokoto (Ancient Sword) Period: a shorter, straight sword used mainly for thrusting,

The katana.

as opposed to slashing and cutting. A little later the sword became longer and curved, to be more effective in battle while its user was on horseback.

- Koto (Old Sword) Period: a period of renaissance, when skills and craftsmanship took great leaps forward. The swords were very long, designed for use on horseback.
- Muromachi Period: a period of great battles and wars, with sword-making proceeding at a frenzied rate and the quality suffering somewhat. It was during this period that the famous katana emerged, accompanied by a shorter sword called the wakazashi. These two swords were worn only by warriors of the Samurai class.
- Shinto (New Sword) Period: a period of embellishment, during which the swordsmiths went to great lengths to create the finest blades, and also worked on every feature of the sword with the utmost consideration and detail. Many of these swords are rare and extremely beautiful, and have ended up in museums and private collections.
- Modern Period: in 1868 the Meii Emperor passed a law forbidding anyone to wear a sword, although he did allow a small number of swordsmiths to continue to make swords, in order to preserve the ancient arts. During the Second World War many historic swords were destroyed or confiscated. Many 'officers' swords' existed around this time, but they were simply manufactured from forged steel, and bore no resemblance to the swords

produced in the true tradition of the art form of the katana.

Katana and Wakizashi

The best known of the swords are the katana and the wakizashi. The latter was the smaller of the two and worn underneath the katana. It was intended to be used with one hand and, even though the katana would be removed during house calls, the wakizashi would always be worn.

Sai

The sai consists of steel or iron rod, a long hilt, and a square hook coming out from the rod about a hand's width from the base or the hilt. There were many variations, and examples have been found with wrist guards (tsuba). The weapon could be carried either hanging from a belt, in a scabbard, or hanging from the wrist, tied by a cord on the weapon's hilt.

When held correctly, the sai was designed to cover the length of the forearm. Carried by the police of the times, it was useful and effective in defence against other swords, including the Samurai sword, and could easily kill or maim an opponent. It could be used to parry or block, or to trap and disarm another swordsmen when used by a skilled practitioner.

The sai strikes with more power when used with a punching action, or backwards, when used as an elbow strike.

Although there is a certain amount of

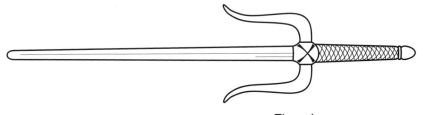

The sai.

debate on the subject, some believe that the sai was originally an agricultural tool, used by farmers to measure the distance between seeds in a crop. It was poked into the ground, or dragged along, using its forked shape to leave three holes or lines. It therefore allowed the farmer to line up his crops evenly. There is no doubt that, after years of twisting, turning, flipping and even throwing this 'tool', the farmer would become quite adept at handling it.

It is difficult to say when the sai was first introduced to the public but in 1968 *Black Belt* magazine published an article on the Okinawan Sai. This weapon became an instant sensation. Imports at the time were of very poor quality, made of pot metal, which resulted in many people making or commissioning their own. Some of the oldest sai from China date back over 100 years and were made of forged iron.

War Fan

These fans were used in many ways. In a social context, they were used by young maidens to hide their blushes, but they also

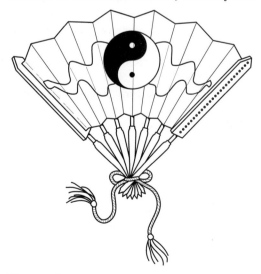

The war fan.

evolved into a very versatile piece of the Samurai armoury. It could be used as a shield, as a parrying implement or as a striking weapon. The fans were manufactured from various materials but the war fans were usually made of metal.

Bo or Staff

Said to have derived from a farming tool called a tenbib ('tin-beeb'), the bo (pronounced 'bow') was a wooden staff that was used for carrying buckets or bundles. The weights were attached to each end and the person carrying them rested the centre of the shaft at the base of his neck. His arms would then overlap the staff to create stability.

The bo came in various sizes, from the length of a spear shaft to much shorter. The rokushakumarubo ('roh-ku-shah-ku-mah-ruh-boh'), a 2m long piece of round wood, was said to be the most common. The kaku bo was a four-sided bo that was designed for better grip, while the reasoning behind the rokaku bo (six-sided bo) and the hakkaku bo (eight-sided bo) is unclear. Some argue that it gave the bo more strength as well as a better grip. The Okinawan Bo is tapered at both ends.

Anyone wielding this weapon utilizes all of its length. The most traditional way of gripping the bo as a weapon involves two hand positions: honte mochi ('hon-teh moh-chee'), which is a natural grip, and gyaku mochi ('gah-koo moh-chee'). In honte mochi, the lead hand has its palm facing upwards and the back-hand palm is facing downwards. In gyaku mochi ('gah-koo moh-chee'), the palms are facing in the same direction, either down or up. When blocking, the ends of the bo can be used to parry

The bo or staff.

and deflect. The middle third can be used to block an attack. When striking, the full length of the bo can be used, or just both ends.

The Japanese practised assiduously with this weapon. Although it was not a weapon of nobility, many Ju-jitsu schools incorporated training with it into their curriculum. It was usually made from a very hard, dense wood that would withstand a lot of abuse. After successfully defending himself, the warrior would employ the bo as a striking weapon, using the blunt ends in a jabbing fashion or swinging the entire bo at the opponent, with devastating effect.

Kama

The sickle (kama), originally developed from a farming implement, was also a very efficient weapon in combat. There were various forms of kama. The kama-yari was the simplest, consisting of a handle and a blade forged at right-angles into it. Its blade could be folded rather like a modern-day penknife

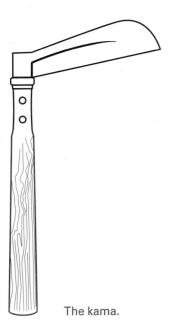

The kama.

and then a ring was used to keep the blade in place. There were larger versions.

The kama could be used to block and parry and to entrap an opponent's weapon, while killing in a scything motion or hacking motion.

Tonfa

Originally thought to have been developed from rice-polishing and grinding implements, the tonfa consisted of two pieces of hardwood. Today, it can be made of various hardened materials such as wood, metal or carbon fibre, and consists of arm-length shafts with a perpendicular hand grip.

The tonfa.

Tonfa are generally used in pairs. In combat, the tonfa can be swung forward for strikes, utilizing both sides of the shafts. The exponent can also perform punch-like movements and whirling motions. Perhaps the most surprising attribute of the tonfa is its ability to go immediately from defence to attack weapon. The weapon covers the user's forearm, protecting against attacks from every conceivable angle. The individual construction of the tonfa means that it can be used to parry or block an opponent's attack, and deliver a devastating counter to a vulnerable area instantaneously.

For some, it is the perfect weapon, but it is very difficult to master. The intricacies of its use call for long and arduous training.

Nunchaku

Made from just two simple pieces of wood, joined with leather, horsehair or chain, the

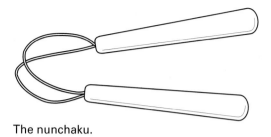

The nunchaku.

nunchaku could be used to capture an attacker's arm, leg or weapon. It could also be whirled around the head and then used to rain blows against the adversary.

Potentially a formidable weapon, the nunchaku has to be used with great caution at the beginning of training. Enthusiastic novices often swing the weapon around carelessly and only end up hitting themselves over the head, or knocking the ends of their fingers back as they attempt to control it. The nunchaku can be whirled around in many varied patterns of movement, creating a defensive shield around the exponent. At the opportune moment he can strike out at his attacker with devastating accuracy. He can also use the weapon to disarm an opponent.

Modern types of nunchaku are still simple in design, consisting of two short bars connected by a length of chain, rope or nylon cord. The chain type is very effective in demonstrations as it swivels more easily.

The nunchaku in its present form is essentially a weapon of Okinawan origin, but there are many different accounts relating to its ancient history. It is likely that there is an element of truth in all of them. The more recent history of the weapon is better known, as it has been popularized by Bruce Lee in several movies.

Why did these weapons appear in the first place? The Japanese occupiers of Okinawa had a tyrannical grip on the population and banning the possession of bladed weapons was another tactic enabling them to consolidate their power. As a result, it seems that the people turned to their simple farming tools as a means of defending themselves. It is believed that many of these tools were adapted and modified for use as weapons, yet were still able to perform their original function.

The nunchaku was probably developed from the rice flail and the horse bit, and took some inspiration from the design of jointed weapons from China. One of the weapons used by the Chinese was the three-section staff and it could be that the nunchaku was modified into a two-section staff.

Defences against Weapons

When defending against a weapon, the simplest, most effective method should always be applied. A weapon attack also allows you to focus fully on the weapon. It is an unusual attack when someone with a weapon strikes you with his other hand first.

To defend against an overhead attack with a club (see p.104), the defender uses a blocking parrying action to deflect the attack to the side. She is now able to execute a shoulder arm lock by trapping her opponent's arm under her blocking arm.

Alternatively, the defender can block and parry the attack the other way (see p.104). She sweeps her other arm into action to effect a figure 4 lock (see p.105) and brings the weapon in against the attacker's own head or throat.

The third possibility against an overhead attack with a club is to use an upper rising block (see p.105), taking the arm backwards by pushing up the elbow and pulling the attacker's arm down with her other hand.

Attacks with edge weapon are the most dangerous, requiring strict vigilance at all

First type of defence against an overhead attack with a club.

Shoulder arm lock after the attack.

Alternative defence against an overhead attack with a club.

Figure 4 lock.

Third defence against an overhead attack with a club.

times. There are no perfect defences against knives; however, it is worth practising some of the basic techniques.

In the face of a lunging attack (see p.106), the defender has stepped out to the side of the attack and blocked down hard on the weapon arm. This is then followed quickly by a kick to the attacker's knee, disabling him.

Protecting himself against a stabbing

Defence against a lunging attack.

Defence against a stabbing attack.

Arm lock and take-down.

attack (see opposite), the defender has managed to grab the attacker's wrist. He steps swiftly to the side as the attacker continues to push against him. He is then able to strike to the attacker's jaw with his elbow, while retaining some control of the hand that holds the knife.

An arm and shoulder lock may also be used against a stabbing attack (see p.108). The defender grabs the attacker's wrist, continuing his movement and pressure, and sweeps the attacker's arm to one side, raising his own leg off the floor. He then takes him to the ground, locking his arm and shoulder.

Joint locking is a very important skill when defending against weapon attacks. Examples include shoulder arm locks and wrist, elbow and arm locks. Being able to strike a vital area (see p.108 for these) after a rapid block is equally important.

When attacked from behind, the defender twists to the side and strikes with the tip of his elbow into the attacker's solar plexus, with a back elbow strike. His other arm is

Shoulder arm lock.

107

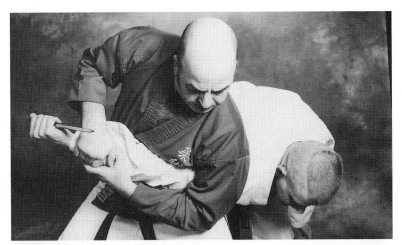

Shoulder arm lock.

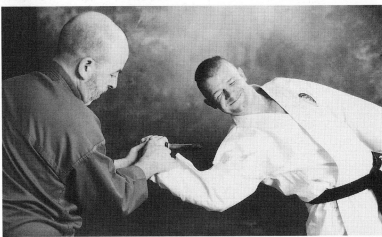

Wrist, elbow and arm lock.

Striking a vital area.

used against his fist to make the strike doubly effective. This weakens the attacker and once the defender has struck the vital area he is able to quickly take up the position of a 'dropping version of body a drop throw'.

Defending against an attack from behind.

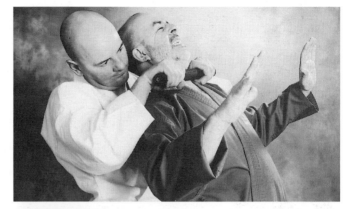

Back elbow strike.

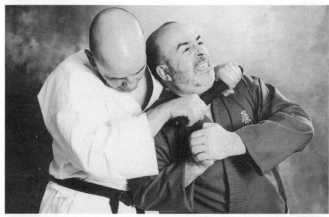

Dropping version of a body drop throw.

11 Competition

It has always been difficult to formulate Ju-jitsu competition as the experienced Ju-jitsu exponent has the ability to render an opponent helpless or injured. It was necessary to devise formats that took all elements of combat, and allowed competitors to use the Ju-jitsu skills in which they had been trained, and to place those formats in a controlled environment.

Striking or attacking vital areas in any way had to be prohibited. Basically, the atemi ('a-the'mee'), Japanese body strikes, are banned. Atemi was a method of attacking an opponent's pressure points and one of the foundation stones of the original combat systems that are classified as Ju-jitsu. The term is now used by most contemporary martial artists when referring to all striking techniques (atemi waza).

Below is a complete breakdown of the rules in competition (by kind permission of the JJIF).

JJIF Fighting System

Section 1 The Fighting System
JJIF's Fighting System is composed of 3 parts:

Part 1 Blows/strikes and kicks.
Part 2 Throws, take-downs, locks and strangulation.
Part 3 Floor techniques, locks and strangulation.

The fighting time per match is divided into 2 rounds of 2 minutes each with a break of 1 minute in between.

Section 2 Weights
Women	0–55 kg
	55–62 kg
	62–70 kg
	70– kg
Men	0–62 kg
	62–69 kg
	69–77 kg
	77–85 kg
	85–94 kg
	94+ kg

Section 3 Competition Area and Organization
a. The competition area for each contest shall be 8 x 8m plus a 1-m wide warning area plus a 1-m wide safety area.
The total contest area shall thus be 12 x 12m.
b. The whole area shall be covered with a Ju-jitsu/Judo tatami. The colour of the warning area shall be different to the one of the competition area.
c. The organizer of the competition shall provide: stopwatches, competition belts (1 red and 1 white per competition area), referee armbands, list and administration papers, first aid (ambulance), doctor, scoreboards (placemen tables) and a place for the referees and the technical committee.
d. The table secretariat shall be composed of a minimum of 4 people, including at least

one qualified referee. There may be 2 table referees at the finals if the number of referees allows it and if this can be done at all finals in the tournament.

Section 4 Competition Dressing
The competitors shall wear a good-quality white Ju-jitsu gi, which must be clean and in good order. The competitors shall wear white or red belts. The gi shall be as follows:
a. The jacket shall be long enough to cover the hips and be tied around the waist by the belt.
b. The sleeves shall be loose enough to grip and long enough to cover half of the forearm but not the wrist.
c. The trousers shall be loose and long enough to cover half of the shinbone.
d. The belt shall be tied with a square knot, tight enough to prevent the jacket from being too loose and long enough to go twice around the body and leave about 15cm of the belt on each side of the knot.
e. Female competitors are required to wear a white T-shirt under their gi. Men are not allowed to wear a T-shirt under their gi.
f. The competitors are required to wear soft, short, light hand protectors and shin/instep protectors, as well as jockstrap and mouthpiece. Female competitors may wear chest protection.

Section 5 Personal Requirements
The contestants must have short finger- and toenails and are not allowed to wear anything that may injure or endanger the opponent. A contestant who needs to wear glasses may only wear contact lenses at own personal risk.

Section 6 Position at Start and End of the Match
a. The contestants shall stand facing each other at the centre of the contest area and approximately 2m apart.

b. At the beginning of the match the competitors will make a standing bow first to the mat referee and then to each other.
c. At the end of the match the competitors will make a standing bow first to each other and then to the mat referee.

Section 7 Course of the Match
a. The match begins with Part 1 and the competitors stand facing each other 2m apart.
b. As soon as there is contact between the competitors (by holding the opponent), Part 2 has begun; in this instant only, simultaneous blows/strikes/kicks and gripping (by the same athlete or by both) are allowed. After the beginning of Part 2 this is no longer allowed.
c. Now the competitors continue fighting in Part 2.
d. As soon as one of the fighters is taken down or thrown, the match continues in Part 3.
e. If the contact is lost in either Part 2 or Part 3, the competitors continue the fight as in Part I.
f. In Part 1, if a competitor only rushes towards the opponent without making a technical action or if he/she is dangerous for him/herself (mobobe), a technical penalty will be given and the match will continue in Part 1.
g. The competitors are allowed to remain in the warning area for only a very short moment (about 5 seconds).
h. Throws that start in the competition area are allowed even if the opponent is thrown into the warning area and/or safety area, provided the throw presents no injury risk for the opponent.

Section 8 Referees
The contest shall be conducted by one Mat-Referee (MR) and two Side-Referees (SR). MR and SRs shall be from different coun-

tries than those of the contestants. The two SRs shall also be from different nations.

MR = Mat-Referee
SR = Side-Referee
R = Red belt (competitor)
W = White belt (competitor)

Section 9 Postion and Funtion of the Mat-Referee (MR)

The MR shall stay within the contest area and has the responsibility for the conduct of the match.

Section 10 Postion and Function of the Side-Referees (SR)

The SRs shall assist the MR and shall be situated outside the competition area. The SRs must place themselves along one side of the competition area where they can follow at any time the course of the match as well as possible.

Section 11 Application of Score and Penalties

a. Scores and penalties must be confirmed by the majority of the referees, therefore at least two referees.

b. If the three referees give a score different from each other, the intermediate score prevails.

c. If one of the referees does not see an action, the lower of the two remaining scores prevails.

Section 12 Application of *Hajime* and *Matte*

a. The MR shall announce hajime in order to start the match.

b. The MR shall announce matte in order to stop the match temporarily in the following cases:

1. When one or both contestants go or find themselves outside the contest area.

2. When one or both contestants perform a forbidden act.

3. When one or both contestants are injured or are taken ill.

4. In any other case when the MR finds it necessary (for example, to reset the gi or to deliver judgement).

5. In any other case when one of the SRs finds it necessary and therefore claps his/her hands.

6. Every time contact is lost in either Part 2 or Part 3.

7. To stop the match during a strangulation or lock if the competitor cannot tap by himself, in such case 2 or 3 points are given to the other contestant (see Section 13).

8. When Osae-komi time is over.

c. Every time the MR announces matte the time stops.

Section 13 Points

The contest points are to be recorded by the table secretariat for each contest area.

a. The following points can be given in Part 1:
(Blows/strikes and kicks)

1. An unblocked blow/strike or kick in good balance and control 2 points.

2. A partly blocked blow/strike or kick 1 point.

b. The following points can be given in Part 2:
(Throws, take downs, locks and strangulations)

1. A perfect throw 2 points.

2. A perfect take-down 2 points.

3. A strangulation with tapping 2 points.

4. A lock with tapping 2 points.

5. A not-perfect throw 1 point.

6. A not-perfect take-down 1 point.

c. The following points can be given in Part 3:
(Floor techniques, locks and strangulations)

1. An efficient control, announced as Osae-Komi, up to 20 seconds (the competitor cannot get free).

10 seconds = 1 point
20 seconds = 2 points

2. A strangulation with tapping 3 points.

3. A lock with tapping 3 points.

d. An efficient control started within the fighting time of a round is allowed to continue until termination (even after expiration of the fighting time, i.e., 2 minutes).

e. The target area of the body is from the end of the throat to the groin.

f. All strangulations are permitted except strangulations with the hand.

g. An act is technically valid when the competitor shows the techniques with good balance and with controlled combination before going into the next Part.

Section 14 Settlement of the Match

a. A competitor may win the match before the end of the fighting time by correctly executing 2 or 3 point techniques in each of the three Parts.

b. If there are more than 14 points of difference between the competitors at the end of the first round, the match is over.

c. The competitor who has the most points at the end of the match wins the match.

d. If the competitors have equal points at the end of the match, the competitor who has executed more 2 or 3 point techniques wins the match.

e. If the score is equal both in total points and in 2 or 3 point techniques, the competitors do another round of 2 minutes until the match is settled.

This procedure may be repeated.

Section 15 Application of *Sonomama* and *Joshi*

Sonomama shall be used if the MR must temporarily stop the competitors:

a. To give one or both competitors a warning for passivity;

b. To give one competitor a technical penalty;

c. Any other time the referee finds it necessary.

After *sonomama* the competitors continue exactly in the same position they were when the referee announced *sonomama*.

To actually start again the MR shall announce *joshi*.

Section 16 Light Forbidden Acts

a. If one or both competitors show passivity or commit minor technical infringements.

b. To deliberately go outside the warning area with the whole body (both feet) outside the line.

c. To purposely deliver kicks or punches after the beginning of Part 2, when one or the other competitor has already established a grip.

d. To make any further action after matte has been announced.

e. To deliver blows/strikes or kicks to the leg.

f To deliver blows/strikes or kicks at the opponent if he/she is lying down.

g. To make locks on fingers or toes.

h. To make cross-legged locks around the kidneys.

Section 17 Forbidden Acts

a. The second time a competitor makes a light forbidden act.

b. To make attacks like kicking, pushing, punching and hitting the body of the opponent in a hard way.

c. To purposely throw and/or push the opponent outside the warning area.

d. To disregard the MR's instructions.

e. To make unnecessary calls, remarks or gestures to the opponent, MR or SRs.

f. To purposely make an uncontrolled action.

g. To execute straight punches or kicks toward the head.

Section 18 Heavy Forbidden Acts

a. To apply any action which may injure the opponent.

b. To throw or try to throw the opponent with any lock or strangulation or to make any lock on the neck or spinal column while in movement.

c. To make any locks on the neck.

Section 19 Penalties

a. Light forbidden act = Shido (1 point to the opponent).

b. Forbidden act = Chui (2 points to the opponent).

c. Forbidden act + light forbidden act Chui (2 pts) + Shido (1 pt) = Keikoku (3 pts) = Keikoku (3 points to the opponent).

d. 2 forbidden acts

The winner gets 14 points; the loser gets 0 points = Hansoku-make (loss of the match)

e. If a competitor gets 3 points because of the opponent's fault, this is automatically counted as an Ippon and will be noted in the Part in which the last punishment occurred.

f. The first time a competitor makes a heavy forbidden act he/she loses the match with 0 points and the opponent gets 14 points.

g. The second time a competitor makes a heavy forbidden act (in a tournament) he/she is expelled from the rest of the tournament.

Section 20 Walk-Over and Withdrawal

a. The decision of Fusen-Gachi (win by walk-over) shall be given to any contestant whose opponent does not appear for his/her match (the winner gets 14 points).

b. The decision of Kiken-Gachi (win by withdrawal) shall be given to the contestant whose opponent withdraws from the competition during the match. In this case the withdrawer gets 0 points and the winner gets 14 points or the score he/she already achieved, if higher than 14.

c. If the doctor declares that a competitor is out of the match, he/she is also out of the rest of the competition.

Section 21 Injury, Illness or Accident

a. In every case when a competition is stopped because of injury on either or both contestants, the MR and SRs may permit a maximum time of 5 minutes to the injured contestant(s) for rest (the total rest per contestant in each match shall be 5 minutes).

b. The decision of winner or loser when one contestant is unable to continue because of injury, illness or accident during the match shall be given by the MR and SRs according to the following clauses:

c. Injury:

1. When the cause of the injury is attributed to the injured contestant, the injured contestant shall lose the match with 0 points and the opponent shall get 14 points.

2. When the cause of the injury is attributed to the uninjured contestant, the uninjured contestant shall lose the match with 0 points and the opponent shall get 14 points or the score he/she already achieved, if higher than 14.

3. When it is impossible to attribute the cause of the injury to either contestant, the uninjured contestant shall win the match with the points he/she already achieved and the injured contestant shall lose with 0 points.

4. The doctor (medical practitioner) is to decide whether the injured contestant may continue or not.

d. Illness: Generally when one contestant is taken ill during the contest and is unable to continue, he/she shall lose the contest with 0 points and the opponent shall get 14 points or the score already achieved, if higher than 14.

Section 22 Team Competitions

Team competitions are possible and the rules are the same as for individual competitions.

Section 23 Reserves in Team Competitions

a. Reserves may replace contestants who

have been injured or taken ill.

b. The reserves must be in the same weight class or in a lower weight class than the ones who are to be replaced.

c. Reserves may not replace a disqualified contestant.

d. Reserves must be announced and weighed at the same time as the ordinary contestants.

Section 24 Situations Not Covered by the Rules

Any situation which is not covered by these rules should be dealt with by the Referees of the contest in question, who together come to a decision.

JJIF Duo System

Section 1 the Duo System

The JJIF Duo System is aimed at presenting the defence of one contestant against a number of predetermined attacks from a contestant of the same team. The attacks are divided into 4 groups of 5 attacks each. The defence is completely at the defender's choice.

Section 2 Composition

A couple may be formed without any restriction at all, such as weight, age or grade. It is also possible to change Tori and Uke at any time during the competition. The couple are of course responsible for each other. A couple may consist of 2 men, 2 women or mixed.

Section 3 Competition Area and Organisation

a. The competition area for each contest shall be 8 x 8m plus a 1m wide warning area plus a 1m wide safety area. The total contest area shall thus be 12 x 12m.

b. The whole area shall be covered with a Ju-jitsu/Judo tatami.

The competition area shall be clearly identified.

c. The organizer of the competition shall provide: stopwatches, competition belts (2 red and 2 white per competition area), rubber knife, soft stick (c. 50cm long), jury score tables, records, first aid kit, doctor, scoreboards (placement tables) and a place for the jury and the technical committee.

d. The table secretariat shall be composed of a minimum of 2 people.

Section 4 Competition Dressing

The competitors shall wear a good quality white Ju-jitsu gi which must be clean and in good order. The competitors shall wear white or red belts.

The gi shall be as follows:

a. The jacket shall be long enough to cover the hips and be tied around the waist by the belt.

b. The sleeves shall be loose enough to grip and long enough to cover half of the forearm but not the wrist.

c. The trousers shall be loose and long enough to cover half of the shinbone.

d. The belt shall be tied with a square knot, tight enough to prevent the jacket from being too loose and long enough to go twice around the body and leave about 15 cm of the belt on each side of the knot.

e. Female competitors are required to wear a white T-shirt under their gi. Men are not allowed to wear a T-shirt under their gi.

Section 5 Personal Requirement

The contestants must have short finger- and toenails and are not allowed to wear any thing that may injure or endanger the partner.

A contestant who needs to wear glasses may only wear contact lenses at own personal risk.

Section 6 Position at Start and End of the Contest

a. The competing couples shall stand facing each other at the center of the contest area and approximately 2m apart.

b. At the beginning of the contest the competitors will make a standing bow first to the mat referee and then to each other.

c. At the end of the contest the competitors will make a standing bow first to each other and then to the mat referee.

d. Upon the first attack of each series, Tori shall have the jury on his/her right side; after that the attack may come from either side.

Section 7 Attack Groups

a. The attacks are divided into 4 groups:
1. Gripping attacks;
2. Embracing and neck lock attacks;
3. Punches/blows and kicking attacks;
4. Weapon attacks.
Each group consists of 5 attacks

b. The Mat Referee (MR) draws 3 attacks for each series and then shows these shortly to the active couple before the attack. The other couple will use the same attacks but in another order called by the MR.

c. The feet position is completely up to the competitors.

d. It is allowed to make a shock to break the opponent's balance before the attack.

Section 8 Competition Pocedure

The competition is between two couples. Couple 1 has red belts and couple 2 has white belts.

Couple 1 starts series I and gets its scores, after that couple 2 proceeds with series 1 and gets its scores.

Couple 2 starts series 2 and gets its scores, after that couple 1 proceeds with series 2 and gets its scores.

Couple 1 starts series 3, etc. and couple 2 starts series 4, etc.

This shifting system gives the fairest score distribution and by that the best result for the competitors and the spectators.

Section 9 Drawing of Lots

At drawing of lots the first drawn couple is always red.

Section 10 Mat Referee (MR)

The MR shall remain within the contest area and shall have the responsibility for the conduct of the match.

The MR will use cards to draw the attacks and to help him/herself visualize the attack. He/she should indicate to the jury if the attack is the correct one.

Section 11 Jury

The jury shall consist of 5 licensed referees, each one from a different country.

The jury members give their points upon instruction of the MR by holding their respective score tables over their heads. The tables are taken down on request of the MR.

Section 12 Application of *Hajime* and *Matte*

a. The MR shall announce the number of the attack in order to make the competitors start.

b. The MR shall announce matte in order to stop the competitors.

Section 13 Criteria of Judging

a. The jury shall look for and judge the following :
1. Attitude;
2. Effectiveness;
3. Speed;
4. Control;
5. Powerful attack.

b. The overall score should give more importance to the attack and to the first part of the defence.

Section 14 Norms of Judging

The attacks and defence must follow certain norms:

a. Atemis must be powerful, with good control and given in a natural way considering possible follow-up.

b. Throws and take-downs shall contain opponent balance breaking and be made at good speed and with good balance.

c. Locks and strangulations must be shown to the jury in a very obvious and correct way, with tapping by Uke.

d. Both the attack and the defence shall be executed in a technical and realistic way.

Section 15 Score System

The scores are given from 0 to 10 by each jury member. The highest and the lowest scores are taken away, according to the judging methods of similar competition forms.

Section 16 Giving of Scores

The jury gives scores after each series of 3 techniques and on request of the MR.

Section 17 Walk-Over and Withdrawal

a. The decision of Fusen-Gachi (win by walk-over) shall be given to the competing couple whose opponents do not appear for their match.

b. The decision of Kiken-Gachi (win by withdrawal) shall be given to the competing couple whose opponents withdraw from the contest during the match.

Section 18 Settlement of the Match

If the competing couples have equal points at the end of the match they repeat the match until there is a difference in the overall score achieved at the end of a series. In this second round of competition the MR draws new attacks from his/her cards and the couple with white belts starts series 1, etc.

Section 19 Injury, Illness or Accident

a. When an injury, illness or accident occurs, the active couple has a right to a maximum time of 5 minutes rest before continuing (the total rest per couple in each match shall be 5 minutes).

b. If a couple cannot continue after an injury, Kiken-Gachi is given to the other couple.

Section 20 Team Competitions

Team competitions are possible and the rules are the same as for individual competitions.

Section 21 Situations Not Covered by the Rules

When any situation arises which is not covered by these rules, this should be dealt with by the MR and the jury of the contest in question, who together come to a decision.

The BJJAGB (British Ju-Jitsu Association) also has guidance notes on the various components required for competition.

• The siting of the facility.
• The dojo floor and its markings.
• Internal environment.
• Equipment and storage.
• Provision for Officials and competitors.

The above competition can also be broken down into single elements to encourage enhancement of individual skills.

The elements below are also used as a competition format but not as an International Governing Body Format.

Random Attack

This element allows the practitioner to defend him or herself against virtually any attack. The attacker is shown a technique from a book of hundreds of pictures. These pictures are divided up into the belt grading

Attacks in the Duo System

The feet position is totally free in all attacks.

Series 1
Gripping attacks

Series 2
Embracing and
neck lock attacks

Series 3
Punches/strikes
and kicking attacks

Series 4
Weapon attacks

systems. So if the defender is a green belt the attacks will all come from within the syllabi of green belt and below. The attacker in theory will not be attacked with anything outside his repertoire.

The judges are looking for the most effective and economical defence against the given attack and will mark the competitors accordingly. As the grades get higher the attacks become more numerous and difficult and really test the defender who in a split second has to defend himself against any one attack.

This form of competition is the most realistic, closely resembling an actual self-defence situation.

Ground Fighting

This element of competition allows the fighters to compete and utilize the combative grappling of Ju-jitsu. All joint locks, except on the spine, are permissible, as are strangles and chokes. Senior competitors have to win by submission. As with all types of competition, the safety of the competitor is paramount. Junior rules for ground fighting are different in that the emphasis is to immobilize the opponent using holding techniques as opposed to the locking, strangles and chokes that are used in the Senior sections.

Sparring

An upright fighting contest in which head guards, gloves, shin pads, padded boots, groin, gum and chest protectors protect the competitors.

Points are awarded for the striking of permissible areas using either kicks or punches. However if either competitor manages to take hold of the other, no more strikes of any description can be attempted. They must now try to defeat each other using their Ju-jitsu expertise to throw their opponent to the ground. Again points are awarded for the actual throws.

Kata

It is now better understood that the original kata forms involved learning the striking of vital areas and acupuncture points. The knowledge was not widely available in the West, and there was some misinterpretation of what kata really meant. The type of kata that exists in most martial arts today does not reflect the essence of kata, where the master knows and understands the true application; this has become lost in the term 'traditional moves'.

Kata is a series of pre-arranged moves, performed by one exponent, or with a partner, or with weapons. The idea is that the individual is performing moves against an imaginary opponent. In the past it was an ideal way of learning techniques in the absence of an instructor. Ju-jitsu training methods were originally devised specifically for the development of the warrior, to give him a greater chance of survival on the field of battle, or in a one-to-one situation.

In many Western cultures, there is evidence of great warriors who, mainly due to their wealth, were able to receive a formal education, including training in hand-to-hand and weapon-to-weapon combat. However, nothing compares with the prestige and high-ranking position of the Samurai class in Japan, which continued throughout several generations. As in other upper-class societies, the Samurai were also trained in art, music and the other cultural necessities that were expected at court.

In his training in one-to-one combat and unarmed combat, the warrior needed to be able to practise both with a partner and on his own, and kata was developed from this need. Kata enabled the warrior (or, today, enables the Ju-jitsu student) to practise all aspects of basic Ju-jitsu.

In its original form, kata became very finely tuned, to the extent that the practitioner was able to keep the amount of moves to a minimum against a variety of complex attacks. More recently, kata has become something of an art form and competitions in kata are now common at championships. The judges look for the minutest detail of any misplaced hand, foot, stance, or so on. However, it is important not to lose sight of the fact that the practice of kata was also developed to further the internal spiritual battle of mind and body development.

Ju-jitsu kata are divided up into various elements, from the very basic ones, which allow a novice to learn blocking, striking and kicking, to more complex movements involving the blocking, striking and kicking, as well as breakfalling. The kata are given specific names for the purposes of judging, and they are standard throughout Ju-jitsu. There are also free-form kata, which the student has learned as part of his own association's syllabus.

Useful Terminology

Japanese	English
Jodan	Upper
Gedan	Lower area
Sagete	Lower
Futari	Sitting
Osu	Pull
Owari	Stop (motion)
Ue	Upper part
Mushin	Reaction
Tate	To stand
Dame	Bad
Seiretsu	Line up
Shoshinsa	New student
Bunkai	Working (with one another)
Kudasai	Please wait
Kyusho	Vital point
Chudan	Middle area
Agete	Lift
Tachi	Standing
Seiza	Kneeling
Hiku	Push
Mijikaku	Shorter
Shite	Lower part
Manasu	Let go
Sumimasen	Sorry (floor apology)
Sonkei	Respect
Suki	Gap (distancing)
Gakun	Pulling Grip
Keikorenshu	Exercise
Mudansha	Below black belt
Hann Tachi	Half kneeling
Age uchi	Rising strike
Age uke	Rising block, usually with the forearm
Age tsuki	Rising punch
Ago	Jaw, chin (common usage)
Ai	Love, harmony. The fundamental concept of all the martial arts.
Aiki	Harmonization of mind and body
Ashi	Foot or leg (common usage)
Ashi barai	Leg sweep

Numbers

1	ichí
2	ní
3	san
4	shí
5	gó
6	rokú
7	shichí
8	hachí
9	kú
10	júu
100	hyakú

Pronunciation guide

a	as in *far*
chi	*chee*
e	as in *edible*
go	as in *go*
ha	*haw*
hya	a sound between *hi* and *a*
i	as in *it*
ju	as in *June*
ku	*coo*
n	as in *never*
ni	*knee*
o	as in *coat*
ro	*roe*
sa	as in *sock*
shi	*shee*
u	as in *root*

Foot or Leg Techniques

Hiza guruma
Ouchi-Gari
Osoto-Gari
Sasae-tsurikomi-ashi
Harai-tsurikomi-ashi
Okuri-ashi-harai
Deashi-harai

Kouchi-gari
Kosoto-gari
Kosoto-gaki
Ashi-guruma
Ochi-mata
O-guruma
Osoto-guruma
Osoto-oshi

Useful Adresses and Resources

The American Ju-Jitsu Institute is the oldest Ju-jitsu organization in the USA, formed in 1939 and chartered in 1947. The website, at www.dnvmarketing.com/aji/index.html is a useful educational resource.

Danzen Ryu records are held by Prof. Gary Jones, House of Kodenkan/Chi SooTe Jiu Jitsu, Tanglewood Center, 7509 Cantrell Rd., Little Rock, Arkansas, USA.

The British Ju-Jitsu Association GB
5 Avenue Parade
Accrongton
Lancashire
BB5 6PN

Tel. 0870 774 1122
Fax. 0870 055872
Email.TheChairman@bjjagb.org.uk
www.bjjagb.org.uk

Sport England
16 Upper Woburn Place
London
WC1H 0QP
Tel. 020 7723 1500
Fax. 020 7383 5740

Ju-Jitsu International Federation
(The world's governing body)
General Secretary
Frank Furst
Nippon Sport ApS
Vesterbrogade 173
DK-1800
Frederiksberg
Tel. 45 3323 1313
Fax. 45 3324 0113
email. frank@nippon.dk
www.jjif.web.com

Ju-Jitsu Organizations Worldwide

Andorra
Federacio de Ju-Jitsu d'Andorra
c/Mayor 12, Planta Baja
Andorra La Vella
Andorra

Tel: +376 829 041
Fax: +376 829 707

Angola
Angola Ju-Jitsu Federation
Cidadela Desportiva
C. Postal 18334 Luanda
Angola

Tel: +244 2 362 489
Fax: +244 2 331 578

Argentina
Escuela Argentina de Jiu-Jitsu
Corrientes 155, Dpto. 5, Campana 2804
Prov. de Buenos Aires
Argentina

Tel: + 54 3489 426 926
Fax: + 54 3489 424 913

Australia
Australian Ju-Jitsu Federation
3 Rotorua Court, Aspley
Queensland 4034
Australia

Tel: + 61 (0) 47 3862 9634
Fax: +61 (0) 47 3862 9674

Austria
Ju-Jitsu Verband Österreich
Prager Strasse 20
1210 Wien
Austria

Tel: +43 1 707 89 42
Fax: +43 1 707 89 42

Azerbaijan
Azerbaijan Republic Ju-Jitsu
National Federation
59 Aga-Neymatulla st., Apt. 1
370052 Baku
Azerbaijan

Tel: +99412 64 22 54
Fax: +99412 98 11 00
e-mail: baku_az_jujitsu@hotmail.com

Belgium
Belgishe Ju-Jitsu Federatie
Ligue Belge de Ju-Jitsu
Azalealei 100
2170 Merksem
Belgium

Tel: +32 3 647 2020
Fax: +32 3 647 2020

Bolivia
Primera Asociación Boliviana de
Jiu-Jitsu y Artes Marciales
Casilla 4557
Cochabamba
Bolivia

Tel: +591 4 424 9768
e-mail:theo@albatros.cnb.net

Brazil
Confederación Brasilena de Jiu-Jitsu
Rua Pedro Gomes Cardim 87, Apto. 61
Morumbi, CEP 05.617-000 Sao Paulo
Brazil

Tel: +55 11 377 13991
Fax: +55 11 377 13991

Bulgaria
Ministry of International Affairs, Martial
Arts
1 Vassil Vevsky Str. 088 60 03 22
Sofia 1000
Bulgaria

Tel: +359 88 600 322
Fax: +359 64 410 763

Canada
Yudansha Ju-Jitsu Canada
90 High Street, Collingwood
Ontario L9Y 4K2
Canada

Tel: +1 705 445 3533
Fax: +1 705 429 0419
e-mail: bartons@look.ca

Chile
Associacion Chilena de Jiu-Jitsu
Valentin Letelier 79
Linares
Chile

Tel: +56 73 213 688
Fax: +56 73213 688

Denmark
Dansk Judo og Ju-Jitsu Union
Broendby Stadion 20
2605 Broendby
Denmark

Tel: +45 4326 2920
Fax: +45 4326 2919
e-mail: dju@dju.dk

Finland
Suomen Karateliito, Section Ju-Jutsu
Radiokatu 12
00240 Helsinki
Finland

Tel: +358 (9) 0 158 2319
fax: +358 (9) 0 148 1654

France
Federation Française Judo et Ju-Jitsu, D.A.
43 Rue des Plantes
75680 Paris Cedex 14
France

Tel: +33 1 40 52 1637
Fax: +33 1 40 52 1670

Georgia
Georgian Ju-Jitsu Federation
25/85 Mitskevitch Street
380094 Tbilisi
Georgia

Tel: +995 32 375 451
Fax: +995 32 942 546

Germany
Deutscher Ju-Jutsu Verband e.V.
Bundesgeschäftsstelle
Paul Rohland Str. 2
06712 Zeitz
Germany

Tel: +49 3441 310 041
Fax: +49 3441 213 429

Greece
Hellenic Ju-Jitsu Non Professional Sports
Fan Federation
P.O. Box 15 Koropi
19400 Koropi
Greece

Tel: +30 1 662 4579
Fax: +30 1 662 3260

Hungary
All Union of the Hungarian Martial Arts
Dozsa Gy.ut 1-3
1143 Budapest
Hungary

Tel: +36 1 180 3634
Fax: +36 1 686 619

India
Ju-Jitsu Federation India
New Ashiwad, Flat no. 3, Sai Baba Park
Evershine Nagar Malad (W), Mumbai 400
064
India

Tel: +91 22 880 3217
Fax: +91 22 881 8326

Iran
Iranian Ju-Jitsu Association
P.O. Box 13185-1687
Teheran

Iran

Tel: +98 21 750 5619
Fax: +98 21 623 6642

Israel
Israel Ju-Jitsu International Federation
P.O. Box 44789
Haifa
Israel

Tel: +972 4 8672 435
Fax: +972 4 8304 322

Italy
Associazione Italiana Ju-Jitsu e D.A.
Via Ines Negri 80/1
17012 Albissola Mare (Savona)
Italy

Tel: +39 019 82 27 86
Fax: +39 019 82 73 92

Japan
All Japan Ju-Jitsu Federation
1-21, 1cho, Minamihancho-Nishi
Sakai-City, Osaka 5900967
Japan

Tel: +81 722 24 2154
Fax: +81 722 24 2157

Morocco
Federation Royale Marocaine de judo, Ju-
Jutsu, Aikido
Compl. Sportif Mohammed V
Prt. no. 10 Rue Brahim Nakhai, Maarif,
Casablanca
Morocco

Tel: +212 236 72 11
Fax: +212 239 30 88

Mexico
Federation Mexicana de Jiu-Jitsu
Av. Rio Churubusco Pta. 9
Cd. Deportiva de la Magdalena, Mixhuca
D.F.C.P. 08 010
Mexico

Tel: +52 5 524 70 09
Fax: +52 5 530 22 34

Netherlands
Judo Bond Nederland
Postbus 7012
34030 JA Nieuwegein
Netherlands

Tel: +31 (0) 30 603 8114
Fax: +31 (0) 30 604 4323

Norway
Norwegian Martial Arts Federation, Jujutsu
Section
Serviceboks 1 U.S.
Sognsveien 75, 0840 Oslo
Norway

Tel: +47 21 02 9000
Fax: +47 21 02 9601

Pakistan
Pakistan Ju-Jitsu Federation
H-8, Opposite C 125, Rehman Pura Colony
Lahore 54600
Pakistan

Tel: +92 42 731 3383
Fax: +92 72 757 8804

Paraguay
Associacion Paraguaya de Jiu-Jitsu
c/Julia M. Cueto 466, c/Sdo. Ovelar Fdo. de
la Mora
Casilla, Correo 1729
Paraguay

Tel: +595 21 511 060
Fax: +595 21 511 060

Poland
Polish Ju-Jitsu Association
ul. Warszawska 11a
40-009 Katowice
Poland

Tel: +48 (0) 32 253 0656
Fax: +48 (0) 32 253 0656

Portugal
Associacao de Jiu-Jitsu de Portugal
Rua da Fabrica 11

Torres Nonas 2351
Portugal

Tel: +351 249 813 811
Fax: +351 249 825 863

Puerto Rico
Associacion de Ju-Jitsu de Puerto Rico
P.O. Box 203
Vega Alta
Puerto Rico 00.762

Romania
Romanian Martial Arts Federation
Ministry of Youth and Sports
16 Vasille Conta Street, Sect. 2 Bucharest
Romania

Tel: +40 1 321 0495
Fax: +40 1 211 0161

Singapore
Ju-Jitsu Association Singapore
1, Scotts Road
#05-32/33 Shaw Centre
228208
Singapore

Tel: +65 6333 1311
Fax: +65 6338 5272

Slovenia
Ju-Jitsu Federation of Slovenia
Kvedrova Cesta 29, p.p. 102
8290 Sevnica
Slovenia

Tel: +386 63 442 420
Fax: +386 63 481 826

Spain
Federation Espanola de Judo y D.A., section
Jiu-Jitsu
Ferraz 16
Madrid 28008
Spain

Tel: +34 1 559 4876
Fax: +34 1 547 6139
e-mail: info@rfejudo.com

Sweden
Svenska Budoföbundet, section Ju-Jutsu
Idrottens Hus
12 387 Farsta
Sweden
Tel: +46 8 605 6000
Fax: +46 8 604 0010

Switzerland
Schweiz Judo & Ju-Jitsu Verband
Postfach 249
3000 Bern 32
Switzerland

Tel: +41 31 368 05 75
Fax: +41 31 368 05 76
e-mail: office@sjv.ch

Uruguay
Federation Uruguay de Jiu-Jitsu
Casa de los Deportes General, Artigas-
Canelones 978/982
C.P. 11.100 Montevideo
Uruguay

Tel: +598 2 900 6381
Fax: +598 2 902 5107

USA
United States Ju-Jitsu Federation
3816 Bellingham Drive
Reno NV 89511
USA

Tel: +1 775 851 8875
Fax: +1 775 887 8871

Further Reading

Draeger, Donn F., *Classical Budo*, John Wetherhill Inc., New York.
Farkas, Emil, and Corcoran, John, *The Overlook Martial Arts Dictionary*, The Overlook Press, 1983.
Ferrie, Eddie, *Ju-Jitsu*, The Crowood Press, 1990.
Frederic, Louis, *A Dictionary of the Martial Arts*, Charles A. Tuttle Company, Boston, 1988.
Hakao, Seigo, *Japanese-English English-Japanese Dictionary*, Random House, 1995.
Kano, Jigoro, *Kodokan Judo*, Kodansha International, 1994.
Kim, Sun-Jin, Kogen, Daniel, Kontoglannis, Nikolaos, and Wong, Hall, *Tuttle Dictionary of the Martial Arts of Korea,* *China and Japan*, Charles A. Tuttle Company, Boston, 1996.
Kirby, George, *Intermediate Ju-Jitsu*, Ohara, 1985.
Lawler, Jennifer, *The Martial Arts Encyclopedia*, Masters Press, 1996.
Rahming, D'Arcy, *Combat Ju-Jitsu: The Lost Art*, Modern Ju-Jitsu Inc., 1991.
Craig, Darrell Max, *Japan's Ultimate Martial Art*, Charles A. Tuttle Company, Boston, 1995.
Ratti, Oscar, and Westbrook, Adele, *Secrets of the Samurai*, Charles A. Tuttle Company, Boston
Shirato, Ichiro (rev. Hiroko Storm), *Living Language Japanese Dictionary*, Crown Publishers Inc., 1993.

Index